The Maritime Provinces Atlas

by
Robert J. McCalla

Cartographers
Dawn Allen and Peggy McCalla

Maritext

Halifax

Canadian Cataloguing in Publication Data
McCalla, Robert J.
Main entry under title:
The Maritime Provinces Atlas

ISBN 0-921921-05-5
1. Maritime Provinces — Maps.
I. Title

G1120.M32 1988 912' .715 C88-098536-4

The development costs of this book were supported, in part, by a grant from the Canadian Studies program of the Department of the Secretary of State.

PRODUCTION TEAM
Dawn Allen and Peggy McCalla/cartographers
Ingrid Haworth/editorial co-ordinator
Christopher Majka/computer graphics
Paul Sampson/research assistant

The map projection used for the Maritime Provinces in this atlas is Lambert Conformal Conic with Standard Parallels at 49°N and 70°N.

MARITEXT LIMITED
5359 Inglis Street
Halifax, Nova Scotia
B3H 1J4
Maritext is a joint venture of
Formac Publishing Company Ltd., Halifax
Ragweed Press Inc., Charlottetown
David S. Nelson, Rothesay

Printed in Canada.

INTRODUCTION

Welcome to the first comprehensive Maritime Provinces atlas! The pages which follow use maps, graphs and photographs to present the geography of New Brunswick, Nova Scotia and Prince Edward Island. Forty plates, organized in five theme sections, show aspects of the physical and human landscape of the region. Each plate, or two-page spread, is identified with a title, and usually a short statement in a box which describes the contents of that plate.

An atlas can be fun and challenging to use. You can discover facts and relationships you didn't know existed. How long ago were glaciers a feature of this region? Which is the longest river? Where has gas and oil exploration taken place in the offshore area? Do most people live along the coasts? Where are crime rates highest? Which is the most travelled road? What is the most common family name in Cape Breton Island? The answers to these questions and thousands of others can be found in this book. Not only can questions like these be answered, but also answers to questions about the relationships between places and activities can be found. What is the relationship between soil quality and agricultural productivity? Are fish plants located close to fishing grounds? Are the people with the highest incomes found in the cities?

You don't read an atlas; in fact, there is relatively little text to read. Instead, there are maps and graphs to study. Maps are, to some extent, unreal. They are simplifications of reality, meaning that they attempt to show some aspect of the real world on a very small piece of paper. All maps have scales which indicate how much of the world is shown on the map. In this atlas scales are of two types: line scales which show visually how far, say, 100 km is, and representative fractions such as 1: 2 500 000. The interpretation of 1: 2 500 000 is that 1 cm equals 2 500 000 cm or 25 km on the ground. The north arrow on the map is also helpful in relating the map to the real world. Maps contain symbols or patterns which are explained in the legend accompanying each map. If some of the terms are unfamiliar, there is a glossary at the end of the atlas.

The graphs used here are of three types: line, bar and circle. The first two are quite similar except one has lines showing the relationship between the two variables named on the axes, and the other uses bars. The third type of graph is different because it does not have axes. Instead, there is only a circle which is drawn in proportion to the value of the variable being plotted. The legend will tell you the approximate value of the circle. Sometimes the circles will be divided into segments, or pieces of pie, with the size of each segment representing the amount of the entire circle which is contained in that segment category.

A Gazetteer of the Maritimes follows the thematic plates. There is an index to make it easier to find many of the small communities which do not otherwise show up on a small map of the region. The style of these maps is much like a road map with an extensive legend to show you the way.

The information on which the maps and graphs are based comes from a variety of sources and represents the most up-to-date that was available at the time of collection. In most cases, maps and graphs have dates indicating the year represented in the visual material. A full listing of published sources is provided at the end of the book. Space does not permit listing all of the individuals who provided unpublished information, interpreted data or reviewed manuscript maps. However, to all of you, thank you. Also, I wish to express my appreciation to the production team, who through their skill, diligence and determination have created a truly remarkable volume displaying the geography of the Maritime Provinces. Of course, any errors or omissions are my responsibility, and should be reported to the publisher in order to correct them in any subsequent printings or editions.

Robert J. McCalla

TABLE OF CONTENTS

THE WORLD, CANADA AND THE MARITIME PROVINCES PLATE 1

Canada Facts

Surface area: 9 970 610 sq. km making Canada the second largest country by area in the world. The land area is 9 215 430 sq. km; the freshwater area is 755 180 sq. km

The length of the coastline, including that of major and minor islands, is estimated to be 223 734 km, making it the longest in the world.

The highest elevation is Mount Logan, Yukon at 5951 m

The most southerly point is Middle Island, Lake Erie, Ontario at 41° 41' N. The most northerly point is Cape Columbia, Ellesmere Island, NWT at 83° 07' N. The most easterly point is Cape Spear, Newfoundland at 52° 37' W. The most westerly point is the Yukon-Alaska boundary at 141° 00' W.

The population is 25 309 331 (1986)
The population density is 2.8 persons/sq. km

Canada became a nation on July 1, 1867 with the Confederation of Ontario, Quebec, New Brunswick and Nova Scotia. Today Canada consists of ten provinces and two territories. They are, with their dates of joining Confederation:

Province or Territory	Date
Ontario	1867
Quebec	1867
New Brunswick	1867
Nova Scotia	1867
Manitoba	1870
Northwest Territories	1870
British Columbia	1871
Prince Edward Island	1873
Yukon	1898
Saskatchewan	1905
Alberta	1905
Newfoundland	1949

National Capital: Ottawa, Ontario
National Motto: *A mari usque ad mare* : "From sea to sea"
National Animal: Beaver

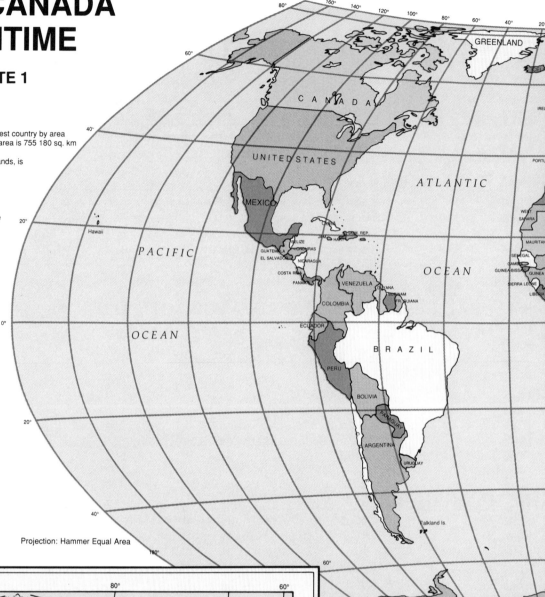

Projection: Hammer Equal Area

West from Gree

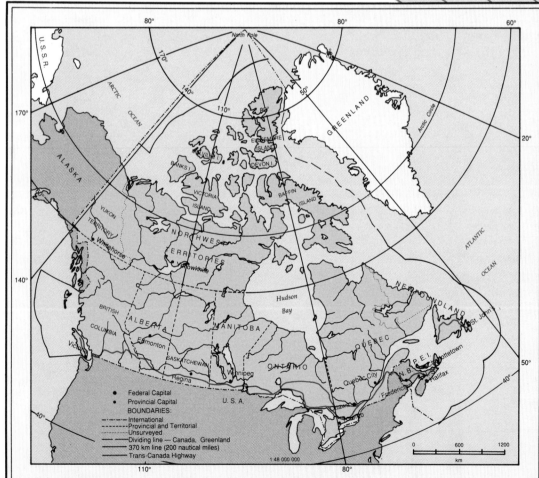

Maritime Provinces Facts

The most northerly point is Dalhousie Island, New Brunswick at 48°
The most southerly point is Cape Sable , Nova Scotia at 43° 23' N
The most easterly point is Cormorandière Rocks, Nova Scotia at 59°
The most westerly point is along the Rivière St-Francis which forms boundary between Maine and New Brunswick at 69° 03' W

New Brunswick
Capital: Fredericton
Population: 709 442 (1986)
Population density: 9.9 persons/sq. km
Total surface area: 73 440 sq. km
Land area: 72 090 sq. km
Freshwater area: 1350 sq. km
Highest elevation: 820 m at Mount Carleton
Length of coastline: 1524 km
Provincial motto: *Spem Reduxit* : "Hope was restored"
Provincial flower: Purple violet

Nova Scotia
Capital: Halifax
Population: 873 176 (1986)
Population density: 16.5 persons/sq. km
Total surface area: 55 490 sq. km
Land area: 52 840 sq. km
Freshwater area: 2650 sq. km
Highest elevation: 532 m at 46° 42' N 60° 36' W (unnamed point)
Length of coastline: 5934 km
Provincial motto: *Munit Haec et Altera Vincit* : "One defends and the other conquers"
Provincial flower: Mayflower

Prince Edward Island
Capital: Charlottetown
Population: 126 646 (1986)
Population density: 22.4 persons/sq. km
Total surface area: 5660 sq. km
Land area: 5660 sq. km
Freshwater area: negligible
Highest elevation: 142 m at 40° 20' N 63° 27' W (unnamed point)
Length of coastline: 1107 km
Provincial motto: *Parva Sub Ingenti* : "The small under the protection of the great"
Provincial flower: Lady's Slipper

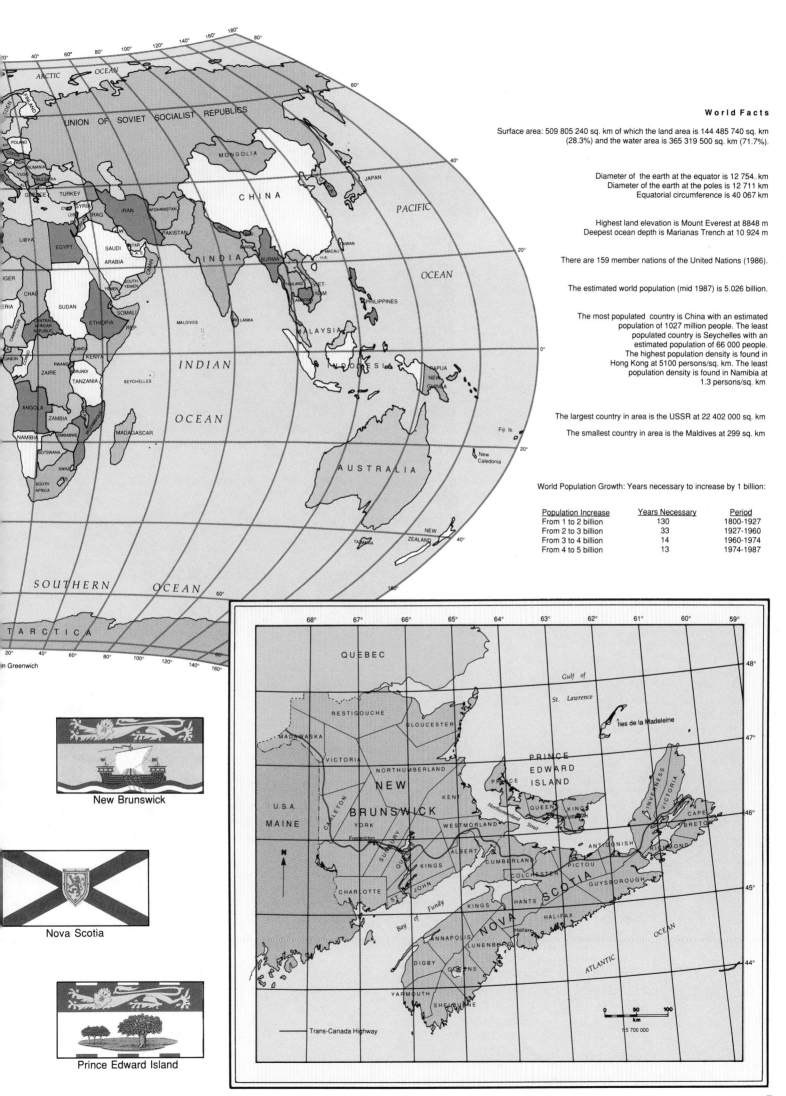

World Facts

Surface area: 509 805 240 sq. km of which the land area is 144 485 740 sq. km (28.3%) and the water area is 365 319 500 sq. km (71.7%).

Diameter of the earth at the equator is 12 754 km
Diameter of the earth at the poles is 12 711 km
Equatorial circumference is 40 067 km

Highest land elevation is Mount Everest at 8848 m
Deepest ocean depth is Marianas Trench at 10 924 m

There are 159 member nations of the United Nations (1986).

The estimated world population (mid 1987) is 5.026 billion.

The most populated country is China with an estimated population of 1027 million people. The least populated country is Seychelles with an estimated population of 66 000 people. The highest population density is found in Hong Kong at 5100 persons/sq. km. The least population density is found in Namibia at 1.3 persons/sq. km

The largest country in area is the USSR at 22 402 000 sq. km

The smallest country in area is the Maldives at 299 sq. km

World Population Growth: Years necessary to increase by 1 billion:

Population Increase	Years Necessary	Period
From 1 to 2 billion	130	1800-1927
From 2 to 3 billion	33	1927-1960
From 3 to 4 billion	14	1960-1974
From 4 to 5 billion	13	1974-1987

New Brunswick

Nova Scotia

Prince Edward Island

THE MARITIME PROVINCES PLATE 2

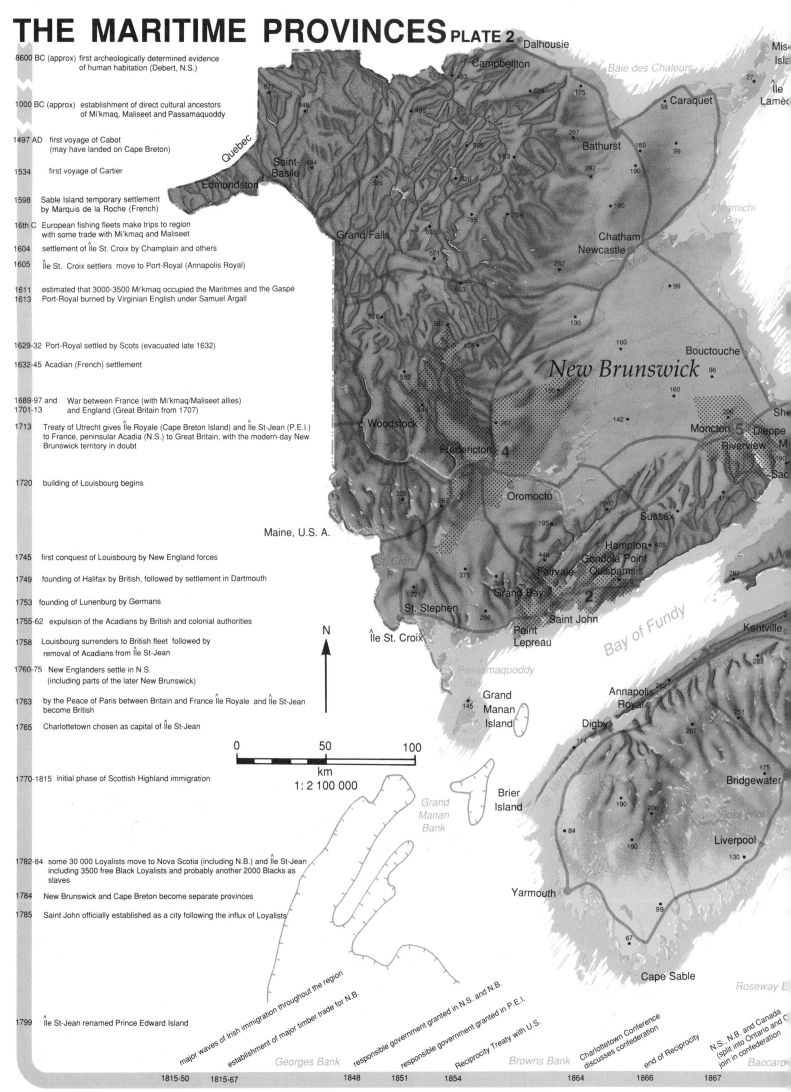

8600 BC (approx) first archeologically determined evidence of human habitation (Debert, N.S.)

1000 BC (approx) establishment of direct cultural ancestors of Mi'kmaq, Maliseet and Passamaquoddy

1497 AD first voyage of Cabot (may have landed on Cape Breton)

1534 first voyage of Cartier

1598 Sable Island temporary settlement by Marquis de la Roche (French)

16th C European fishing fleets make trips to region with some trade with Mi'kmaq and Maliseet

1604 settlement of Île St. Croix by Champlain and others

1605 Île St. Croix settlers move to Port-Royal (Annapolis Royal)

1611 estimated that 3000-3500 Mi'kmaq occupied the Maritimes and the Gaspé
1613 Port-Royal burned by Virginian English under Samuel Argall

1629-32 Port-Royal settled by Scots (evacuated late 1632)

1632-45 Acadian (French) settlement

1689-97 and War between France (with Mi'kmaq/Maliseet allies)
1701-13 and England (Great Britain from 1707)

1713 Treaty of Utrecht gives Île Royale (Cape Breton Island) and Île St-Jean (P.E.I.) to France, peninsular Acadia (N.S.) to Great Britain, with the modern-day New Brunswick territory in doubt

1720 building of Louisbourg begins

1745 first conquest of Louisbourg by New England forces

1749 founding of Halifax by British, followed by settlement in Dartmouth

1753 founding of Lunenburg by Germans

1755-62 expulsion of the Acadians by British and colonial authorities

1758 Louisbourg surrenders to British fleet followed by removal of Acadians from Île St-Jean

1760-75 New Englanders settle in N.S. (including parts of the later New Brunswick)

1763 by the Peace of Paris between Britain and France Île Royale and Île St-Jean become British

1765 Charlottetown chosen as capital of Île St-Jean

1770-1815 initial phase of Scottish Highland immigration

1782-84 some 30 000 Loyalists move to Nova Scotia (including N.B.) and Île St-Jean including 3500 free Black Loyalists and probably another 2000 Blacks as slaves

1784 New Brunswick and Cape Breton become separate provinces

1785 Saint John officially established as a city following the influx of Loyalists

1799 Île St-Jean renamed Prince Edward Island

N

0   50   100
km
1 : 2 100 000

major waves of Irish immigration throughout the region — 1815-50
establishment of major timber trade for N.B. — 1815-67
responsible government granted in N.S. and N.B. — 1848
responsible government granted in P.E.I. — 1851
Reciprocity Treaty with U.S. — 1854
Charlottetown Conference discusses confederation — 1864
end of Reciprocity — 1866
N.S., N.B. and Canada (split into Ontario and join in confederation — 1867

Quebec
Saint-Basile
Edmundston
Grand Falls
Woodstock
Fredericton
Maine, U.S.A.
Oromocto
St. Stephen
Île St. Croix
Point Lepreau
Passamaquoddy Bay
Grand Manan Island
Brier Island
Grand Manan Bank
Georges Bank
Dalhousie
Campbellton
Baie des Chaleurs
Caraquet
Bathurst
Chatham
Newcastle
Miramichi Bay
New Brunswick
Bouctouche
Moncton
Dieppe
Riverview
Sussex
Hampton
Gondola Point
Quispamsis
Fairvale
Grand Bay
Saint John
Bay of Fundy
Kentville
Annapolis Royal
Digby
Bridgewater
Liverpool
Yarmouth
Cape Sable
Roseway
Browns Bank
Baccaro

Population centre
● > 40 000
● 10 000 - 40 000
● 5 000 - 9 999
· 2 500 - 4 999
△ Others noted in time line

⊡ Census Metropolitan Area (C.M.A.)
⊡ or Census Agglomeration (C.A.)

—··—··— International boundary
- - - - - Provincial boundary
—— Main highways
⌢⌣ 200 metre bathymetric contour
· 175 Spot elevations (metres)

1 - Halifax C.M.A.
2 - Saint John C.M.A.
3 - Charlottetown C.A.
4 - Fredericton C.A.
5 - Moncton C.A.
6 - Sydney C.A.

Gulf of St. Lawrence

Prince Edward Island

Lennox Island

·50
·96
Summerside
·142
3 · Sherwood
Charlottetown
·81
·134

Northumberland Strait

·eanors

·herst ·69

·190
Springhill
·328 ·373
Debert ·367
·175
Truro ·267
Westville ·343
Pictou
Trenton
New Glasgow ·328
Stellarton ·312
·236
Antigonish
·236
·221
·160 Nova Scotia
·221
·257
·236

·30
·le
Windsor
·236
ower Sackville
Bedford
1
Halifax Dartmouth
·138

·urg

a Have
Bank

Cabot Strait

St. Pauls Island

Cape Breton Island
·465
·526
·404 ·493 ·480
Margaree
·434
Sydney Mines
North Sydney ·465
Westmount
Baddeck ·343
·238
·328

New Waterford
Glace Bay
6 Sydney
·130
Louisbourg

Bras d'Or Lake

Pictou Island

St. Georges Bay

Port Hawkesbury ·282
·206 ·114
Île Madame

Chedabucto Bay ·114

Strait of Canso

St. Marys R.

Misaine Bank

Canso Bank

Middle Bank

Sable Island ·26

Atlantic Ocean

Sambro Bank

Western Bank

Emerald Bank

Timeline (right side):

1988 referendum in P.E.I. votes in favour of a fixed crossing with N.B.
1977 declaration by Canada of the 370 km (200 nautical mile) offshore limit
1975-83 construction of the Maritimes only nuclear power plant at Point Lepreau, N.B.
1972 foundation of the N.B. Parti Acadien
1971 formation of the Maritime Council of Premiers
1969 creation of federal Department of Regional Economic Expansion (DREE) to assist regional economic development
1960's major outmigration from Maritimes to Ontario and western provinces
1958 Springhill mine disaster
1955 Canso Causeway completed
1939-45 World War II makes Halifax a major staging area for wartime convoys
1930 new U.S. tariffs cut off markets for Maritime resource industries
1922-25 coal and steel strikes in Cape Breton
1922 women's suffrage in P.E.I.
1920-27 "Maritime Rights Movement"
1920-26 collapse of Maritime industrial economy
1919 women's suffrage in N.B. (although women could not run for office until 1934)
1918 women's suffrage in N.S.
1917-27 prohibition implemented in N.B.
1917 Halifax Explosion, the largest man-made explosion prior to Hiroshima
1910-29 prohibition implemented in N.S. (Halifax exempt until 1917)
1909 flight of the Silver Dart at Baddeck
1906-48 prohibition fully implemented in P.E.I. (since 1900 in Queens County only)

Timeline (bottom):

·73 P.E.I. joins confederation
1870s-1920s many Maritimers migrate to "the Boston states"
1876 completion of the Intercolonial Railway linking the Maritimes to Quebec and Ontario
1878 Saint John is fourth largest port of registry of world merchant shipping fleet
1880-1900 high rates of industrial growth in some parts of the Maritimes, but gradual decline of wooden shipping and shipbuilding industries
1881 first Acadian convention at Memramcook
1895-1914 first major wave of takeovers of Maritime industries by outside capital

LANDFORM REGIONS AND GLACIATION PLATE 3

CROSS-SECTION FROM CAMPBELLTON, N.B. TO CAPE SABLE, N.S.

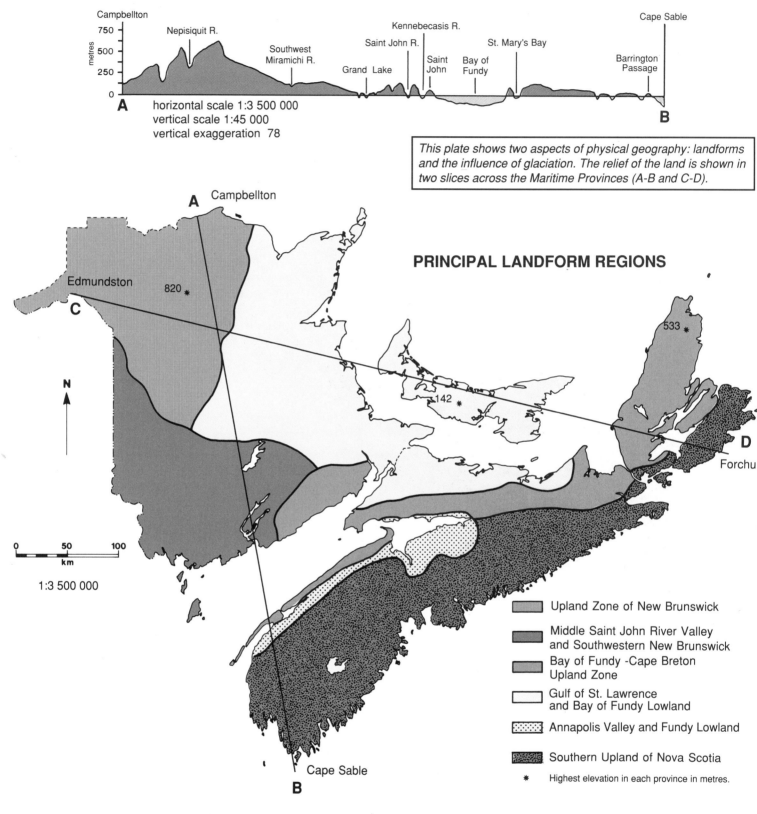

horizontal scale 1:3 500 000
vertical scale 1:45 000
vertical exaggeration 78

This plate shows two aspects of physical geography: landforms and the influence of glaciation. The relief of the land is shown in two slices across the Maritime Provinces (A-B and C-D).

PRINCIPAL LANDFORM REGIONS

1:3 500 000

Upland Zone of New Brunswick

Middle Saint John River Valley and Southwestern New Brunswick

Bay of Fundy -Cape Breton Upland Zone

Gulf of St. Lawrence and Bay of Fundy Lowland

Annapolis Valley and Fundy Lowland

Southern Upland of Nova Scotia

* Highest elevation in each province in metres.

CROSS-SECTION FROM EDMUNDSTON, N.B. TO FORCHU, N.S.

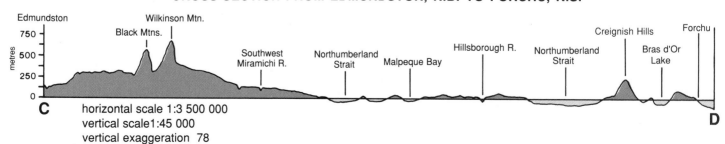

horizontal scale 1:3 500 000
vertical scale 1:45 000
vertical exaggeration 78

THE LAST GLACIAL RETREAT IN EASTERN CANADA

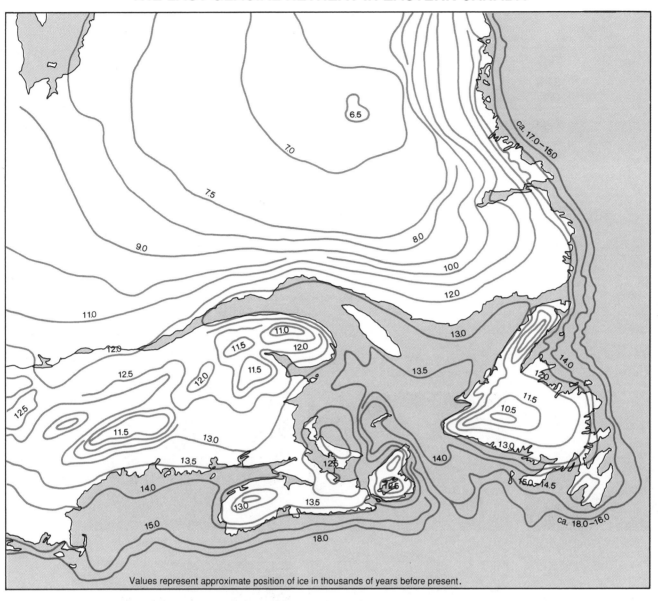

Values represent approximate position of ice in thousands of years before present.

GLACIAL EFFECTS ON LANDFORM

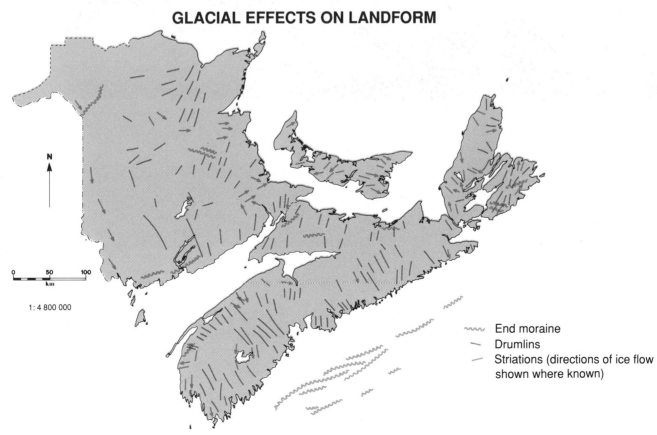

N

0   50   100
km

1 : 4 800 000

〰〰 End moraine
⁓ Drumlins
― Striations (directions of ice flow shown where known)

GEOLOGY PLATE 4

This plate shows the underlying rock types with a table to interpret the geologic history. The location of fossil fuels is shown on the maps at the bottom.

Distinctive features	Million years before present		Geologic period	Rock type	Example
Recent glaciation altered the appearance of the landscape.	1-65		TERTIARY	Sedimentary	Siltstone, mudstone
Sedimentary rock formation under conditions for the creation of oil and gas deposits.	65-140		CRETACEOUS	Sedimentary	Sandstone, siltstone
	140-190		JURASSIC	no representative rocks	
Formation of the Bay of Fundy and the Annapolis Valley including North Mountain.	190-230		TRIASSIC	Sedimentary, some extrusive igneous	Sandstone, shale limestone, basalt
Sedimentary rock formation with coal (Minto, Sydney), potash (Sussex), peat (northeast N.B., P.E.I.) and fossil remains (Joggins, Springhill, P.E.I.).	230-280		PERMIAN	no representative rocks	
	280-345		CARBONIFEROUS	Sedimentary	Sandstone, shale, minor coal
Volcanic activity, both intrusive (N.S. Atlantic Upland) and extrusive (Mt. Carleton).	345-405		DEVONIAN	1.Intrusive igneous	Granite
			DEVONIAN	2.Extrusive igneous	Rhyolite and basalt
			DEVONIAN	3.Sedimentary	Siltstone, sandstone, shale, limestone
Sedimentary rock formation in northern N.B. and the N.S. Atlantic coast with the latter subjected to metamorphism resulting in small and isolated deposits of gold.	405-500		SILURIAN-ORDOVICIAN	Sedimentary and extrusive igneous	Limestone, shale, sandstone and rhyolite
	425-570		ORDOVICIAN-CAMBRIAN	Metamorphic	Slate, schist, greywacke
The oldest rocks in the Maritime Provinces formed along the present shore of the Bay of Fundy.	570-3 500		PRECAMBRIAN	Intrusive and extrusive igneous, deformed	Granite, rhyolite, schist, gneiss

—— — —— Major fault lines

Period	Rock Type
DEVONIAN to CAMBRIAN	Metamorphic and igneous

Period	Rock Type
CARBONIFEROUS to PRECAMBRIAN	Mixed

1 Loading a test cargo of oil from the Scotian Shelf, August 1987.

2 Fossilized amphibian tracks in siltstone, about 340 million years old, Avonport, N.S.

3 Sea stacks at Hopewell, N.B.

4 Mount Carleton, N.B., the highest Maritime Provinces elevation at 820 m.

5 Peat bog and mining at Pointe Sapin, N.B.

6 Sand cliff at Blooming Point, P.E.I.

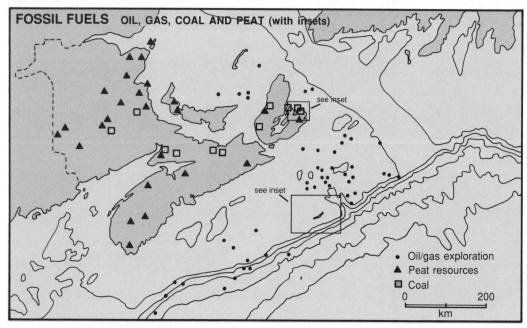

FOSSIL FUELS OIL, GAS, COAL AND PEAT (with insets)

see inset

see inset

- • Oil/gas exploration
- ▲ Peat resources
- ☐ Coal

0 ———— 200
km

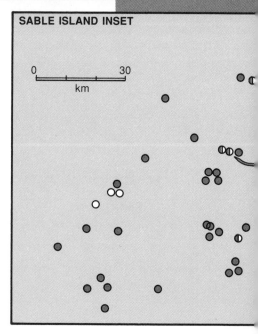

SABLE ISLAND INSET

0 ———— 30
km

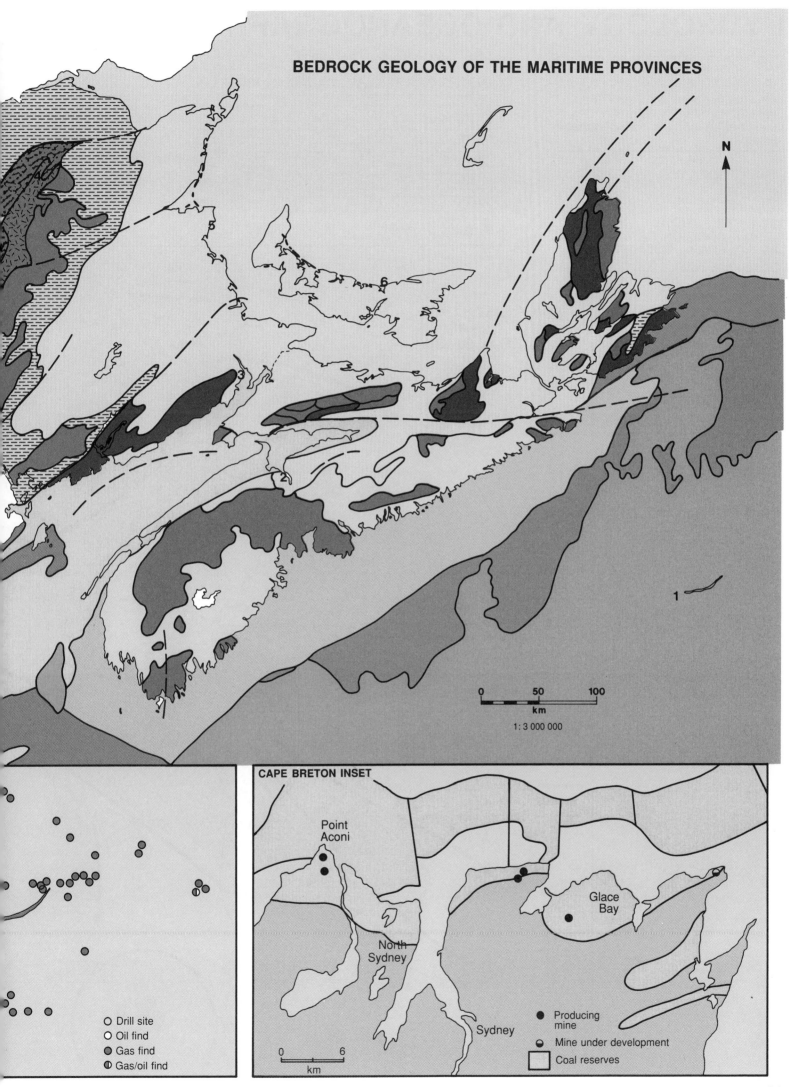

BEDROCK GEOLOGY OF THE MARITIME PROVINCES

N

0   50   100
km
1: 3 000 000

CAPE BRETON INSET

Point
Aconi

Glace
Bay

North
Sydney

Sydney

0   6
km

○ Drill site
○ Oil find
● Gas find
◐ Gas/oil find

● Producing
  mine
◖ Mine under development
☐ Coal reserves

This plate is about water. River discharges in the Maritimes are mapped and graphed (right). Ocean currents and tides are shown for the offshore. Winter ice in the Gulf of St. Lawrence is mapped below.

LENGTHS OF PRINCIPAL CANADIAN RIVERS

River	Length
Mackenzie	4241 km
Yukon	3185 km
St. Lawrence	3058 km
Nelson	2575 km
Ottawa	1271 km
Saint John	673 km

ICE DISTRIBUTION: MEDIAN POSITION OF WINTER ICE COVERAGE (1963-1973)

Dec. 25

Jan. 29

Feb. 26

Mar. 26

May 7

RIVER DISCHARGE, OCEAN CURRENTS AND TIDAL RANGE

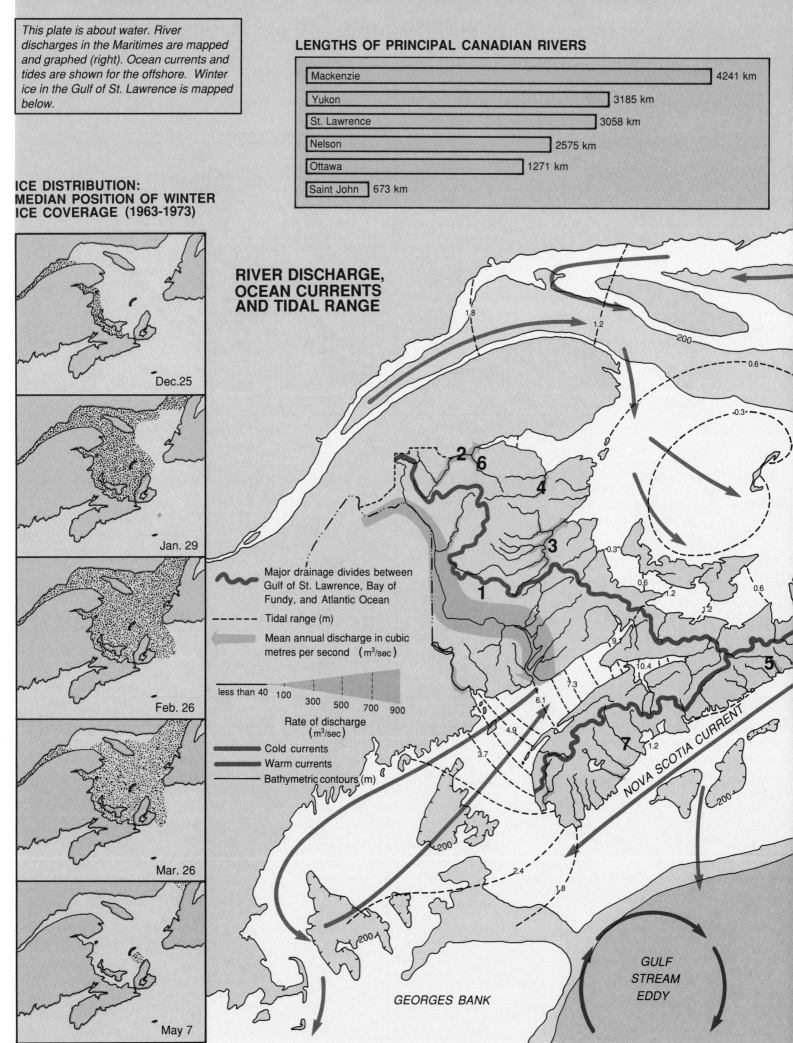

Major drainage divides between Gulf of St. Lawrence, Bay of Fundy, and Atlantic Ocean

Tidal range (m)

Mean annual discharge in cubic metres per second (m³/sec)

less than 40   100   300   500   700   900

Rate of discharge (m³/sec)

Cold currents

Warm currents

Bathymetric contours (m)

NOVA SCOTIA CURRENT

GEORGES BANK

GULF STREAM EDDY

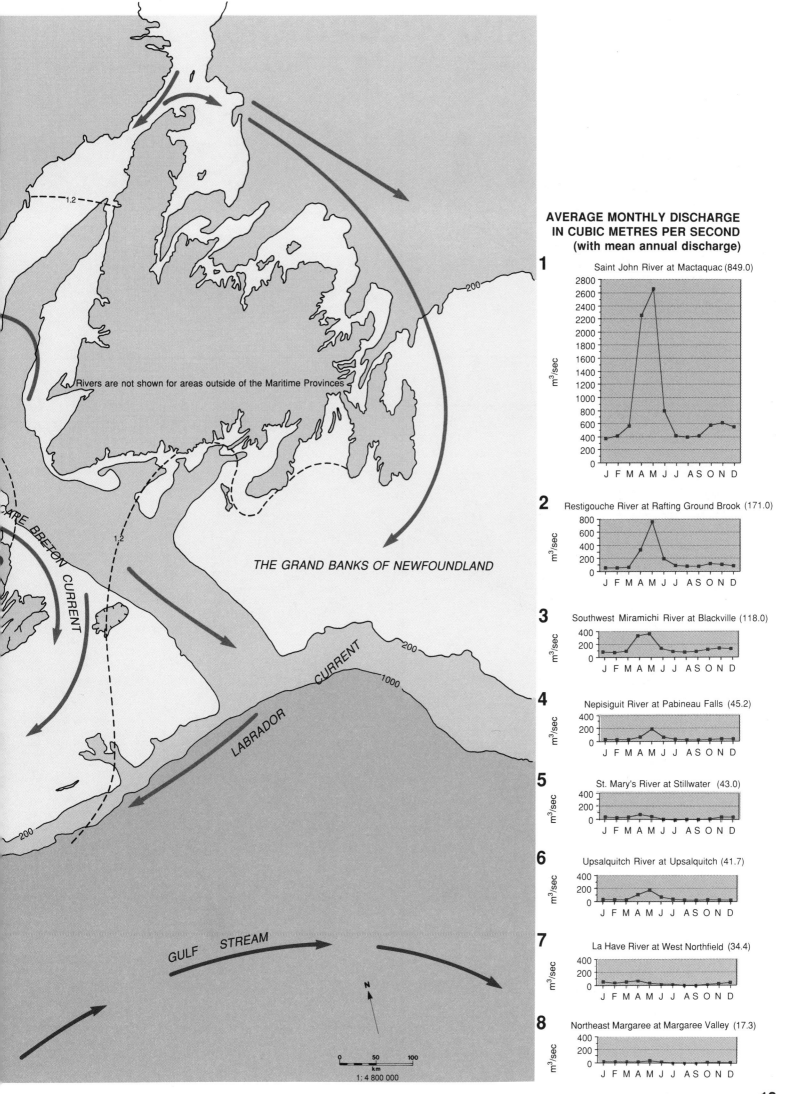

Rivers are not shown for areas outside of the Maritime Provinces

CAPE BRETON CURRENT

THE GRAND BANKS OF NEWFOUNDLAND

LABRADOR CURRENT

GULF STREAM

N

0   50   100
km
1: 4 800 000

AVERAGE MONTHLY DISCHARGE
IN CUBIC METRES PER SECOND
(with mean annual discharge)

1 Saint John River at Mactaquac (849.0)

2 Restigouche River at Rafting Ground Brook (171.0)

3 Southwest Miramichi River at Blackville (118.0)

4 Nepisiguit River at Pabineau Falls (45.2)

5 St. Mary's River at Stillwater (43.0)

6 Upsalquitch River at Upsalquitch (41.7)

7 La Have River at West Northfield (34.4)

8 Northeast Margaree at Margaree Valley (17.3)

TEMPERATURE AND PRECIPITATION PLATE 6

AVERAGE JANUARY AIR TEMPERATURE (°C)

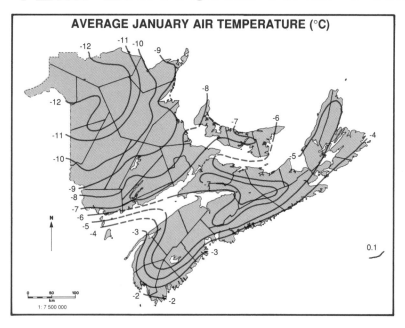

AVERAGE ANNUAL PRECIPITATION (mm)

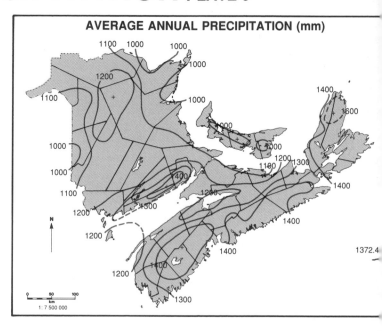

AVERAGE JULY AIR TEMPERATURE (°C)

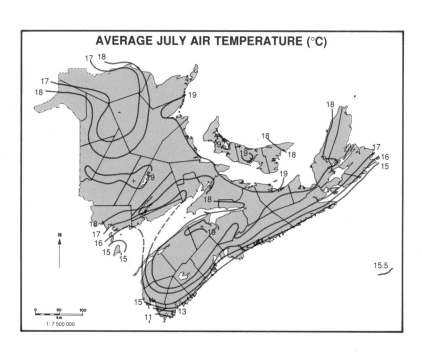

AVERAGE ANNUAL DEGREE DAYS ABOVE 5°C

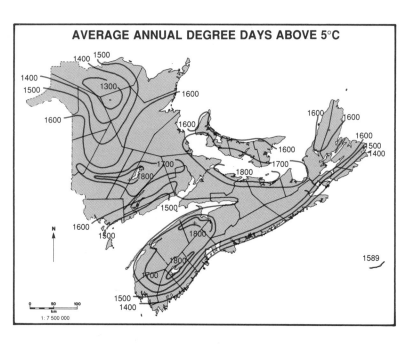

MARITIME CLIMATOLOGICAL STATIONS WITH SELECTED CLIMAGRAPHS

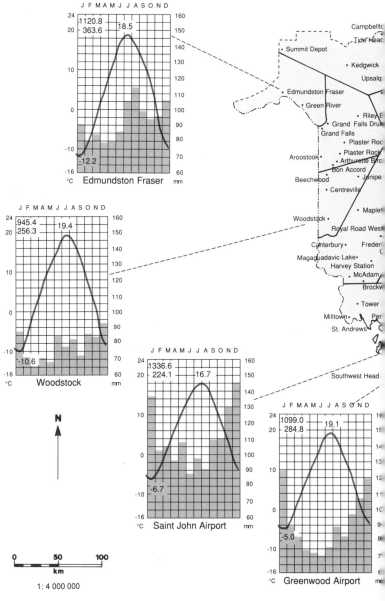

All climagraph values are based on the period 1951-1980.

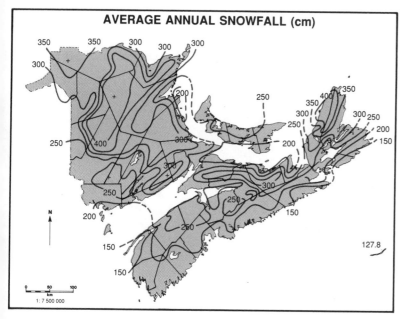

AVERAGE ANNUAL SNOWFALL (cm)

WEATHER FACTS

				Canadian Record
Highest Temperatures (°C)				
N.B.	39.4	Nepisiquit Falls	August 18, 1935	45
		Rexton	August 18, 1935	Midale, Sask
		Woodstock	August 18, 1935	Yellowgrass, Sask
N.S.	38.9	Abercrombie Pt.	August 25, 1976	July 5, 1937
P.E.I.	36.7	Charlottetown	August 19, 1935	
Lowest Temperatures (°C)				
N.B.	-47.2	Sisson Dam	February 1, 1955	-63
N.S.	-41.1	Upper Stewiacke	January 31, 1920	Snag, Yukon
P.E.I.	-37.2	Kilmahumeig	January 26, 1884	February 3, 1947
Greatest Precipitation in 24 hrs (mm)				
N.B.	179.1	Alma	April 1, 1962	489.2
N.S.	238.8	Halifax	Sept 21, 1942	Ucluelet & Brynnor Mines, B.C.
P.E.I.	163.8	Charlottetown	Sept 22, 1942	October 6, 1967
Greatest Precipitation in One Month (mm)				
N.B.	373.4	St George	October, 1926	2235.5
N.S.	570.0	Ingonish Beach	November, 1969	Swanson Bay, B.C.
P.E.I.	315.0	Charlottetown	September, 1942	November, 1917
Greatest Precipitation in One Year (mm)				
N.B.	2149.5	Alma	1979	8122.4
N.S.	2052.6	Spruce Hill Lake	1958	Henderson Lake, B.C.
P.E.I.	1596.7	Alliston	1979	1931
Least Annual Precipitation (mm)				
N.B.	397.5	Dalhousie	1908	12.7
N.S.	518.2	Sable Island East	1918	Arctic Bay, N.W.T.
P.E.I.	470.2	Charlottetown	1924	1949
Heaviest Snowfall (cm)				
N.B.	532.6	Moncton	1974-75	2446.5
N.S.	616.0	Copper Lake	1971-72	Revelstoke & Mt. Copeland, B.C.
P.E.I.	539.0	Charlottetown	1971-72	1971-72

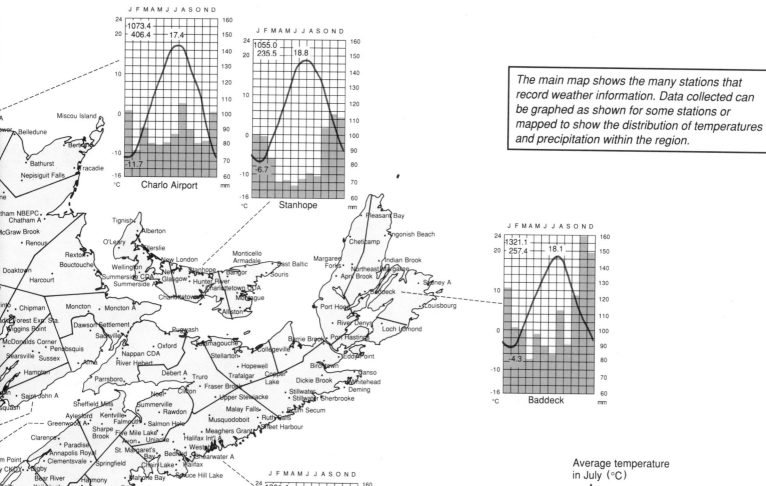

The main map shows the many stations that record weather information. Data collected can be graphed as shown for some stations or mapped to show the distribution of temperatures and precipitation within the region.

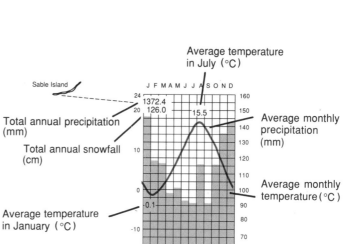

Average temperature in July (°C)

Total annual precipitation (mm)

Total annual snowfall (cm)

Average monthly precipitation (mm)

Average monthly temperature (°C)

Average temperature in January (°C)

FOG, WIND AND WEATHER PLATE 7

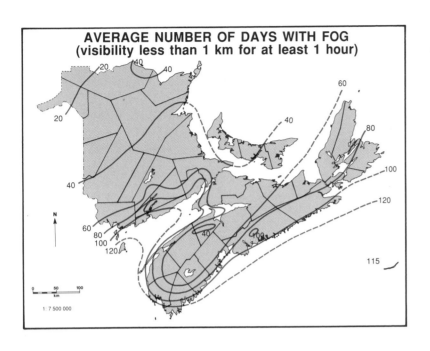

AVERAGE NUMBER OF DAYS WITH FOG
(visibility less than 1 km for at least 1 hour)

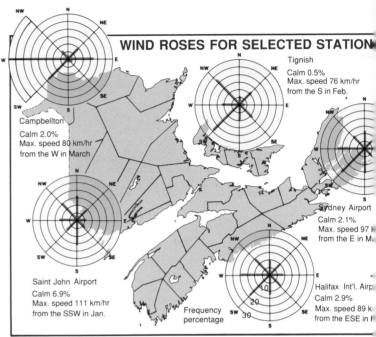

WIND ROSES FOR SELECTED STATION

Tignish
Calm 0.5%
Max. speed 76 km/hr
from the S in Feb.

Campbellton
Calm 2.0%
Max. speed 80 km/hr
from the W in March

Sydney Airport
Calm 2.1%
Max. speed 97 k
from the E in M

Saint John Airport
Calm 6.9%
Max. speed 111 km/hr
from the SSW in Jan.

Halifax Int'l. Airp
Calm 2.9%
Max. speed 89 k
from the ESE in F

Frequency percentage

Fog and wind are distinctive features of the Maritime Provinces (above). The weather is a result of the meeting of different air masses and the creation of warm and cold fronts as shown below. An example of one storm is given on the right.

ATMOSPHERIC CIRCULATION OVER NORTH AMERICA

Arctic airmasses

strongest Westerlies

Tropical airmass

meeting of airmasses

0   1000   2000   3000
km

TWO TYPES OF ATM

warm air

WARM FRONT
about 1200 kilome

cold air

direction of movement

16 THE MARITIME PROVINCES ATLAS

WEATHER MAP FOR FEBRUARY 22, 1986 at 4:00 p.m.
An intense low pressure cell lies off the Nova Scotian coast

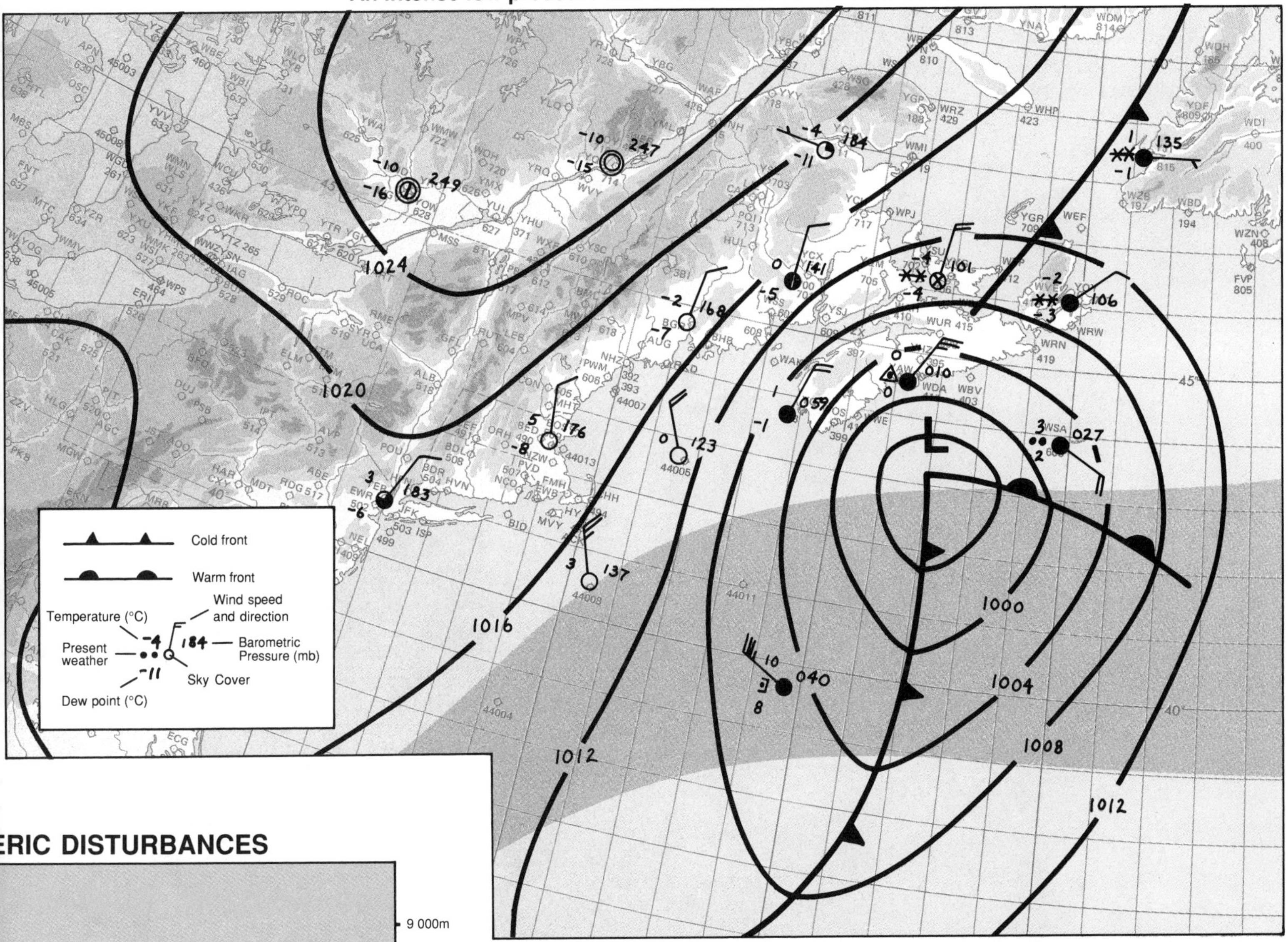

Legend:

▲▲ Cold front

●● Warm front

Temperature (°C)
Wind speed and direction

Present weather

−4 / 184 — Barometric Pressure (mb)

−11 Sky Cover

Dew point (°C)

1024
1020
1016
1012
1008
1004
1000

L

...ERIC DISTURBANCES

9 000m
6 000m
3 000m
0 m

cool air

...ady rain

direction of movement

10 000m

warm air

5 000m

...rd... ...ower

COLD FRONT

0 m

650 kilometres

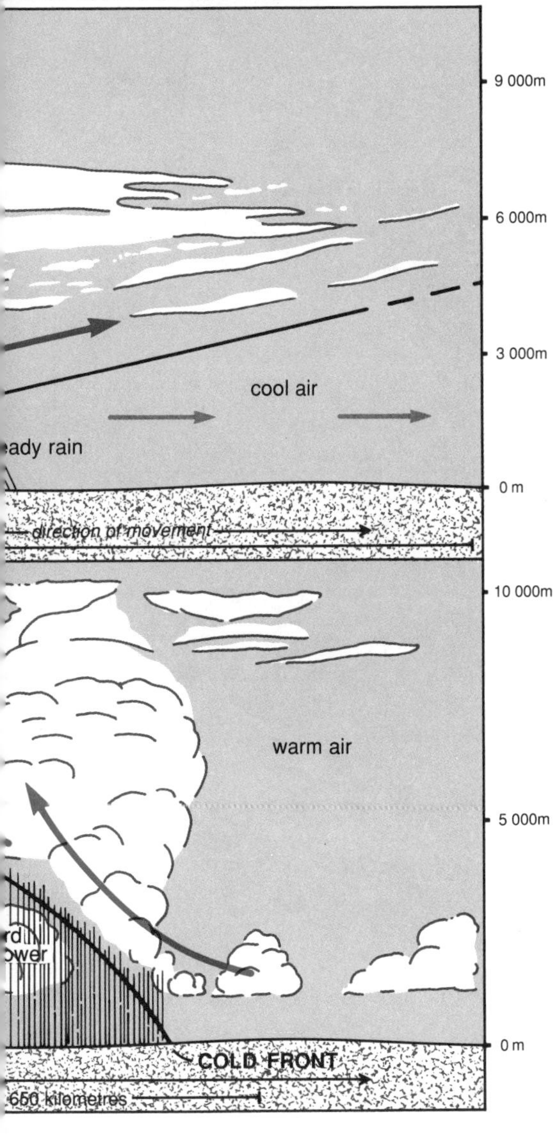

SATELLITE PHOTOGRAPH OF THE ABOVE STORM

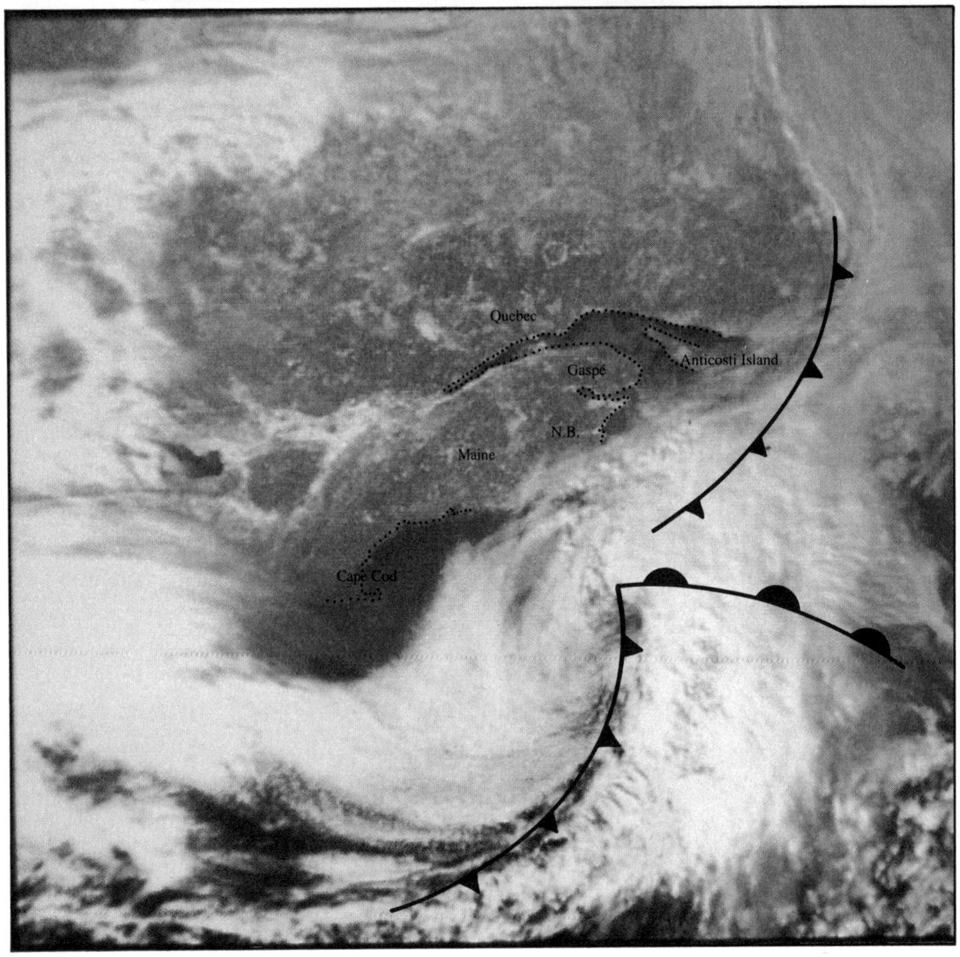

Quebec

Gaspé

Anticosti Island

N.B.

Maine

Cape Cod

ENVIRONMENTAL ISSUES PLATE 8

SENSITIVITY OF SURFACE WATERS TO THE EFFECTS OF ACID PRECIPITATION (1981)

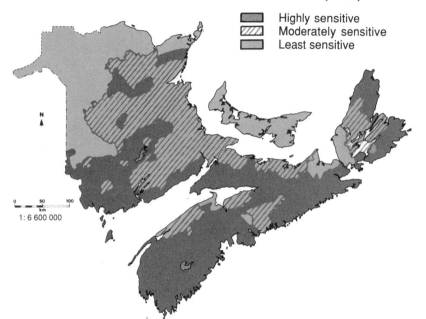

Highly sensitive
Moderately sensitive
Least sensitive

0   50   100
km
1: 6 600 000

MEAN ANNUAL pH OF PRECIPITATION IN EASTERN NORTH AMERICA (1984)

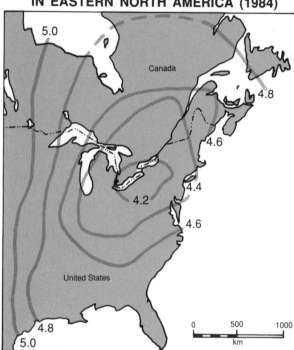

5.0
Canada
4.8
4.6
4.4
4.2
4.6
United States
4.8
5.0

0   500   1000
km

SPRUCE BUDWORM DEFOLIATION IN EASTERN CANADA AND NEW ENGLAND

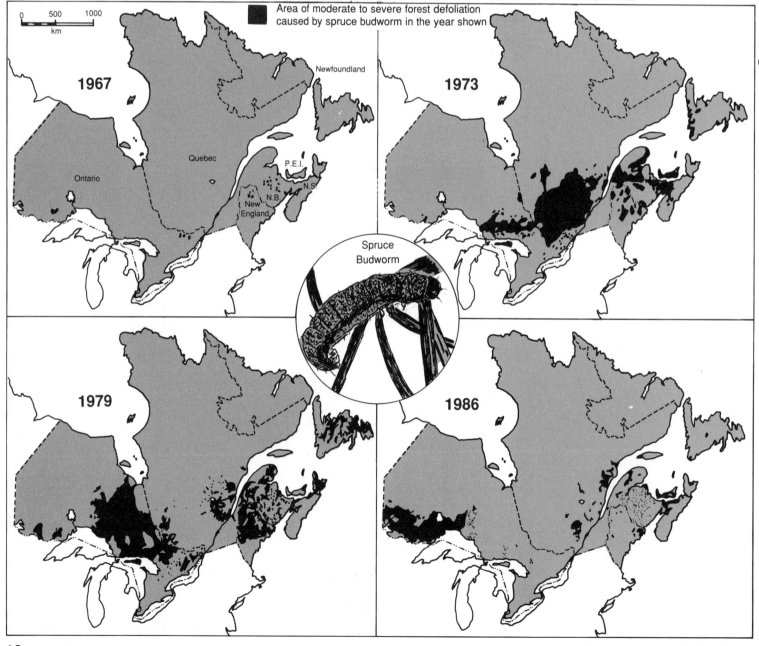

Area of moderate to severe forest defoliation caused by spruce budworm in the year shown

0   500   1000
km

1967

Newfoundland
Quebec
Ontario
P.E.I.
N.S.
N.B.
New England

1973

Spruce Budworm

1979

1986

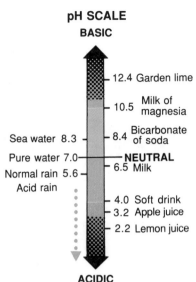

pH SCALE
BASIC

- 12.4 Garden lime
- 10.5 Milk of magnesia
Sea water 8.3
- 8.4 Bicarbonate of soda
Pure water 7.0
- **NEUTRAL**
Normal rain 5.6
- 6.5 Milk
Acid rain
- 4.0 Soft drink
- 3.2 Apple juice
- 2.2 Lemon juice

ACIDIC

Acid rain, forests damaged by spruce budworm and treatment of municipal wastes are issues important to the natural environment. Details on all these issues are shown on this plate.

POPULATION* SERVED BY SEWAGE TREATMENT (1986)			
	N.B.	**N.S.**	**P.E.I.**
Not served	148 649	378 468	4 431
Primary treatment	0	20 000	38 182
Secondary — lagoon treatment	261 278	156 525	15 215
Population	409 927	554 993	57 828

*(people living in villages, towns and cities only)

SEWAGE TREATMENT FOR SELECTED URBAN CENTRES (1986)

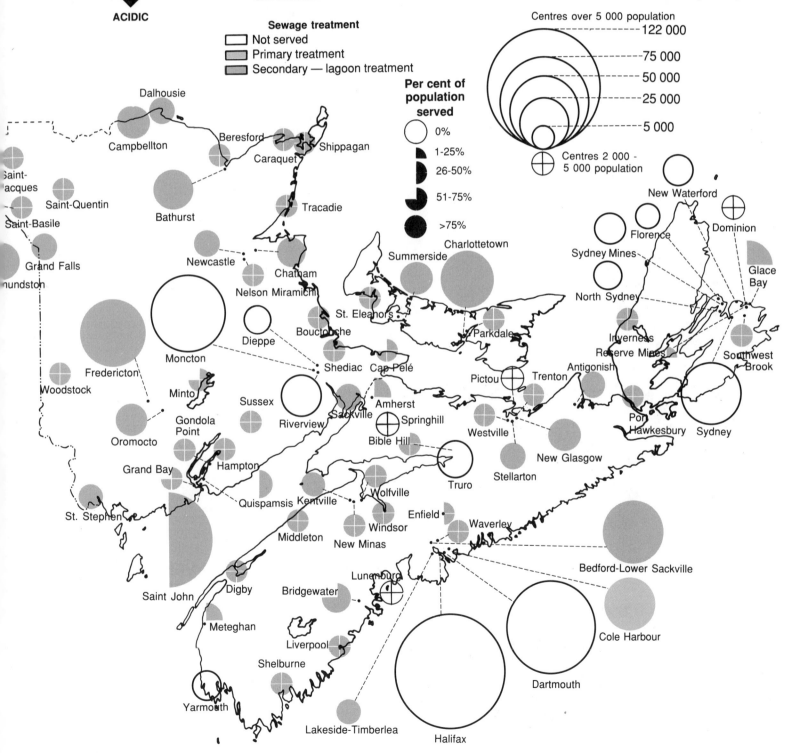

Sewage treatment
- Not served
- Primary treatment
- Secondary — lagoon treatment

Per cent of population served
- 0%
- 1-25%
- 26-50%
- 51-75%
- >75%

Centres over 5 000 population
- 122 000
- 75 000
- 50 000
- 25 000
- 5 000

Centres 2 000 - 5 000 population

SOILS PLATE 9

Soils, their type and potential for agriculture, are shown on this plate. Bar graphs compare the Maritimes with other Canadian regions. The map (far right) and air photograph show details of one good farming area.

Soil type

- Podzolic
- Gray wooded
- Alluvial

Land characteristics

- Dominantly steeply sloping to mountainous
- Significantly stony
- Dominantly well drained with poorly drained areas

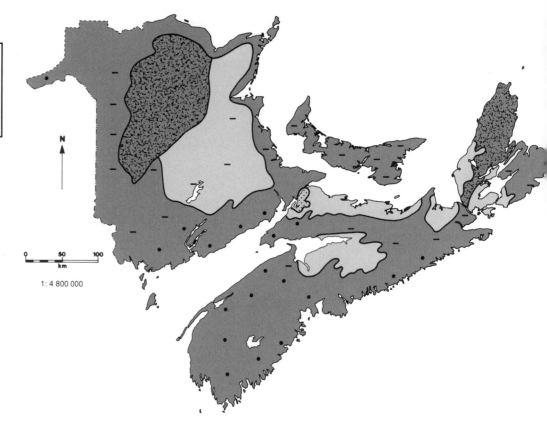

1: 4 800 000

CANADA LAND INVENTORY SOIL CAPABILITY FOR AGRICULTURE

The Canada Land Inventory Soil Capability for Agriculture groups soils into seven classes according to their potential and limitations for agricultura[l] as determined by climate and soil characteristics. Approximately one-third of Canada was surveyed encompassing all the significant land areas capa[ble] of sustained agricultural activities. In the Maritime Provinces only federally owned lands were not classified.

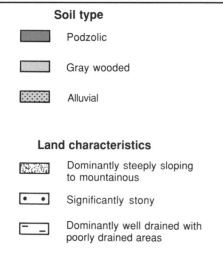

1: 6 600 000

- Good agricultural soils (Classes 1 and 2)
- Limited agricultural soils (Classes 3 and 4)
- Poor agricultural soils (Classes 5, 6 and 7)
- Not classified (federally owned lands)

Class	Degree of limitation	Type of activity supported
EXCELLENT SOILS* **1**	no significant limitations	supports sustained production of cultivated crops
GOOD SOILS **2**	moderate limitations	
FAIR SOILS **3**	moderately severe limitations	
4	severe limitations	marginal for arable culture
5	very severe limitations	supports permanent pasture and hay
POOR SOILS **6**	can support perennial forage crops only	supports wild pasture
7	no capability for arable culture or permanent pasture	

*There are no Class 1 soils in the Maritimes.

DISTRIBUTION OF SOILS ACCORDING TO THE CANADA LAND INVENTORY
CANADIAN REGIONS

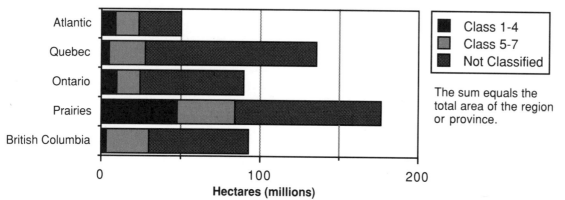

- Atlantic
- Quebec
- Ontario
- Prairies
- British Columbia

0   100   200
Hectares (millions)

- ■ Class 1-4
- ■ Class 5-7
- ■ Not Classified

The sum equals the total area of the region or province.

MARITIME PROVINCES

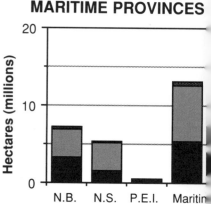

N.B.   N.S.   P.E.I.   Mariti[me]

nsington, P.E.I.   NTS map 11L/5. 1:50 000 (1976). Showing details of the Canada Land Use Inventory Soil Capability for Agriculture in the Kensington
a. 2, 3 and 4 refer to soil class type (see legend on previous page)

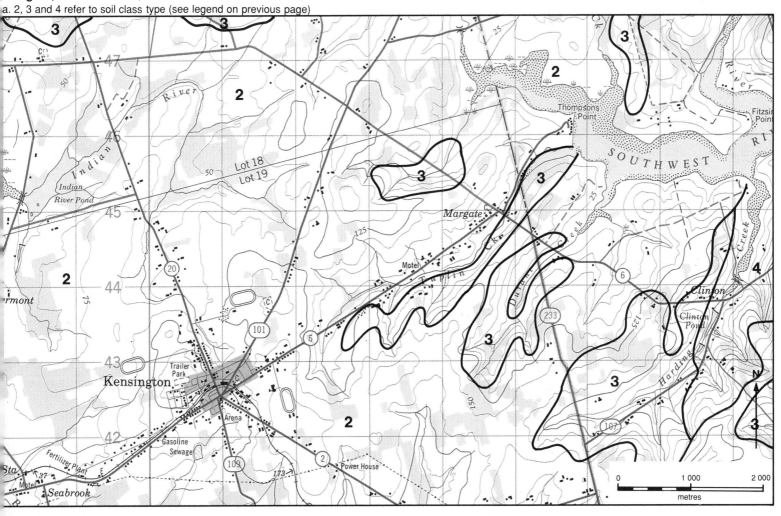

ohotograph, Kensington area. 1:15 625 (1980)

AGRICULTURAL PRODUCTION PLATE 10

AGRICULTURAL ACTIVITY BY TYPE AND PRODUCTION VALUE (1981)

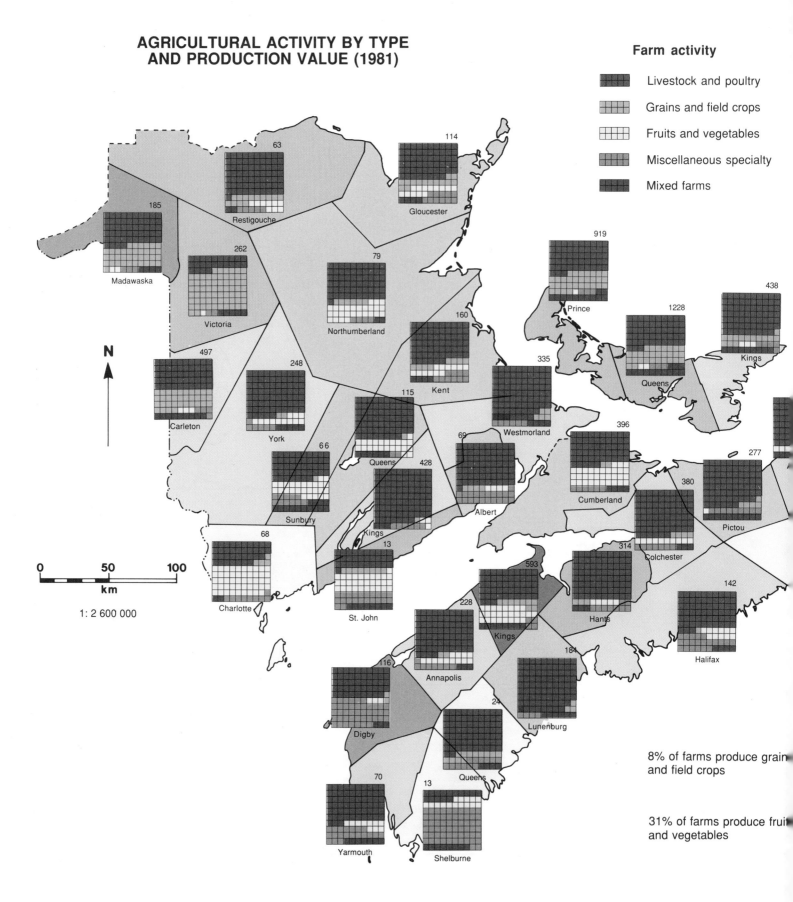

Farm activity

- Livestock and poultry
- Grains and field crops
- Fruits and vegetables
- Miscellaneous specialty
- Mixed farms

1 : 2 600 000

8% of farms produce grain and field crops

31% of farms produce fruit and vegetables

Value of agricultural products sold by total farm area ($ per hectare)

| < $200 | $200-$299 | $300-$399 | $400-$599 | $600-$1000 | > $1000 |

The diversity of farming is shown on the map. Each county is coloured according to the value of products sold. The boxes for each county are divided into 100 squares so that the type and amount of farm activity can be easily read. Other aspects of agriculture are graphed (right).

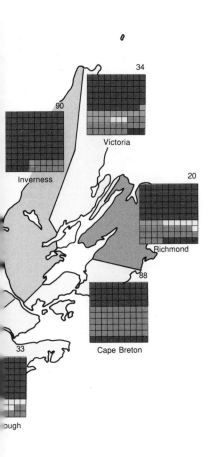

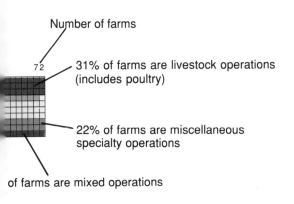

Number of farms

72

31% of farms are livestock operations (includes poultry)

22% of farms are miscellaneous specialty operations

of farms are mixed operations

AVERAGE FARM SIZE AND TOTAL NUMBER OF FARMS, MARITIME PROVINCES

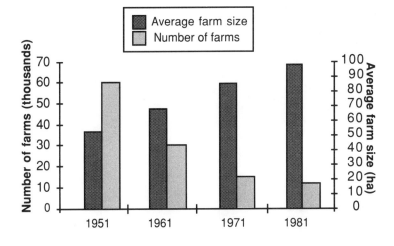

TOTAL IMPROVED FARM LAND

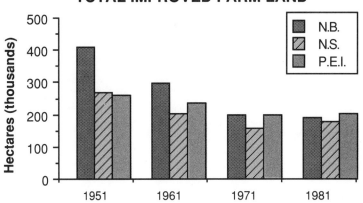

VALUE OF FARM MACHINERY AND EQUIPMENT

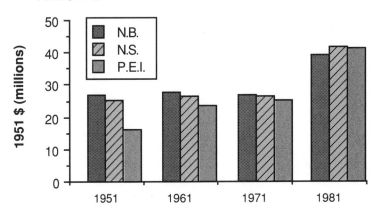

HIRED AGRICULTURAL LABOUR (TOTAL WEEKS OF PAID LABOUR)

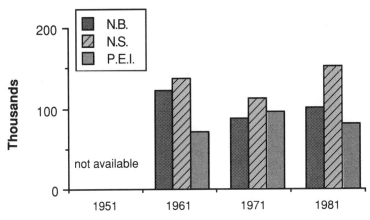

AGRICULTURAL FOOD PROCESSING PLATE 11

PROCESSING PLANTS BY TYPE AND EMPLOYMENT (1986)

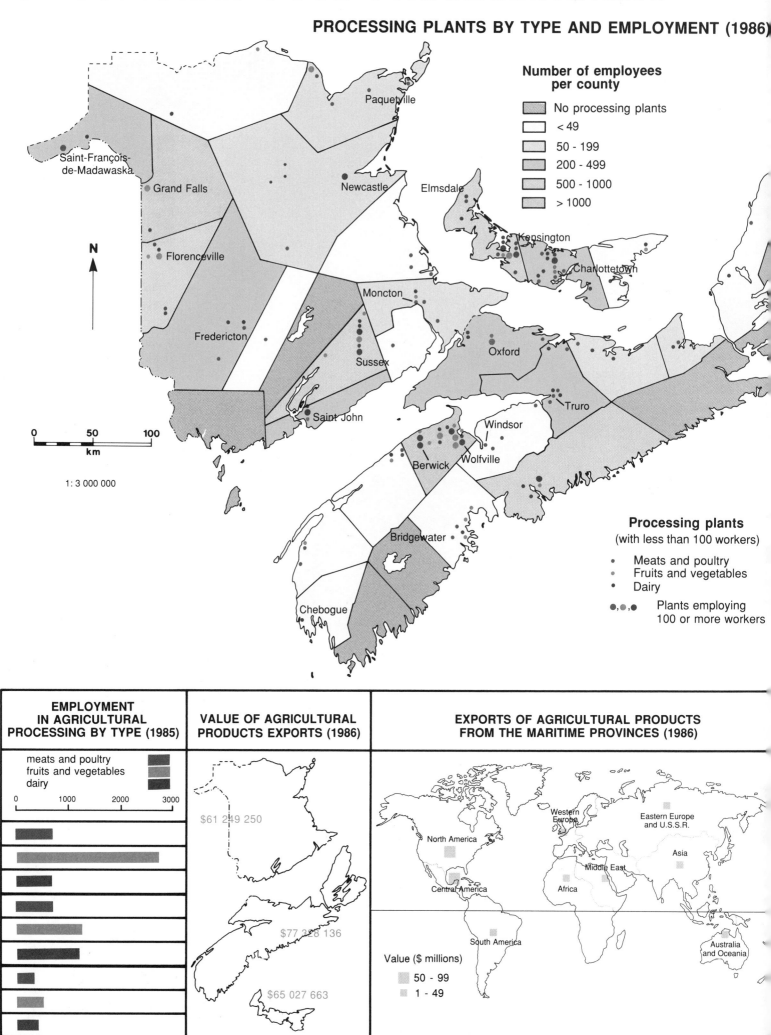

Number of employees per county

- No processing plants
- < 49
- 50 - 199
- 200 - 499
- 500 - 1000
- > 1000

Saint-François-de-Madawaska

Paquetville

Grand Falls

Newcastle

Elmsdale

Kensington

Florenceville

Charlottetown

Moncton

Oxford

Fredericton

Truro

Sussex

Windsor

Saint John

Berwick   Wolfville

Bridgewater

Chebogue

N

0   50   100
km

1 : 3 000 000

Processing plants
(with less than 100 workers)

- Meats and poultry
- Fruits and vegetables
- Dairy

●,●,● Plants employing 100 or more workers

EMPLOYMENT IN AGRICULTURAL PROCESSING BY TYPE (1985)

meats and poultry
fruits and vegetables
dairy

0   1000   2000   3000

New Brunswick

Nova Scotia

Prince Edward Island

VALUE OF AGRICULTURAL PRODUCTS EXPORTS (1986)

$61 249 250

$77 328 136

$65 027 663

EXPORTS OF AGRICULTURAL PRODUCTS FROM THE MARITIME PROVINCES (1986)

Western Europe

Eastern Europe and U.S.S.R.

North America

Asia

Middle East

Central America

Africa

South America

Australia and Oceania

Value ($ millions)
- 50 - 99
- 1 - 49

TOTAL MANUFACTURING SHIPMENTS
FROM FOOD INDUSTRIES (1984)

CANADIAN REGIONS

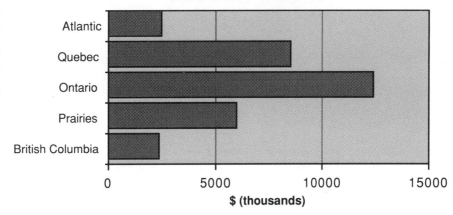

$ (thousands)

MARITIME PROVINCES

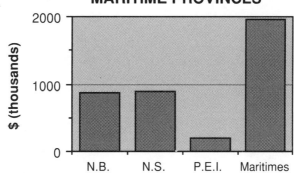

WHOLE MILK UTILIZATION BY PROVINCE (1985),
WITH "MILK SHEDS" FOR NOVA SCOTIA*

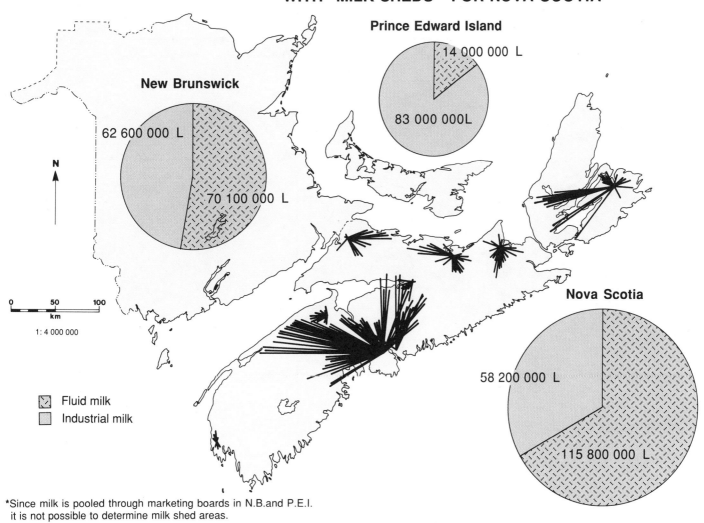

Prince Edward Island

14 000 000 L

83 000 000L

New Brunswick

62 600 000 L

70 100 000 L

N

Nova Scotia

58 200 000 L

115 800 000 L

0   50   100
km

1 : 4 000 000

Fluid milk
Industrial milk

Sydney

*Since milk is pooled through marketing boards in N.B.and P.E.I.
it is not possible to determine milk shed areas.

FISH STOCKS PLATE 12

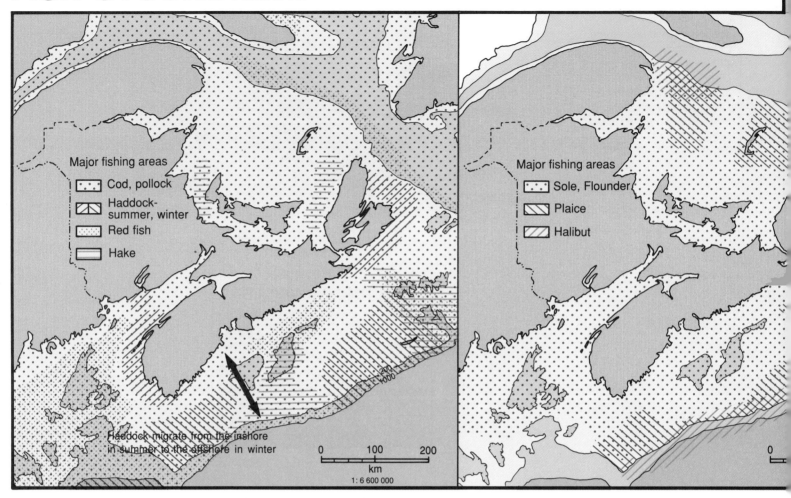

Major fishing areas

- Cod, pollock
- Haddock-summer, winter
- Red fish
- Hake

Haddock migrate from the inshore in summer to the offshore in winter

0   100   200
km
1: 6 600 000

Major fishing areas

- Sole, Flounder
- Plaice
- Halibut

The waters surrounding the Maritimes are productive fish environments. This plate shows the distribution of the important commercial fish stocks. There is also a map of aquaculture operations (bottom right).

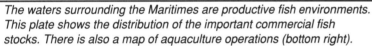

PELAGIC

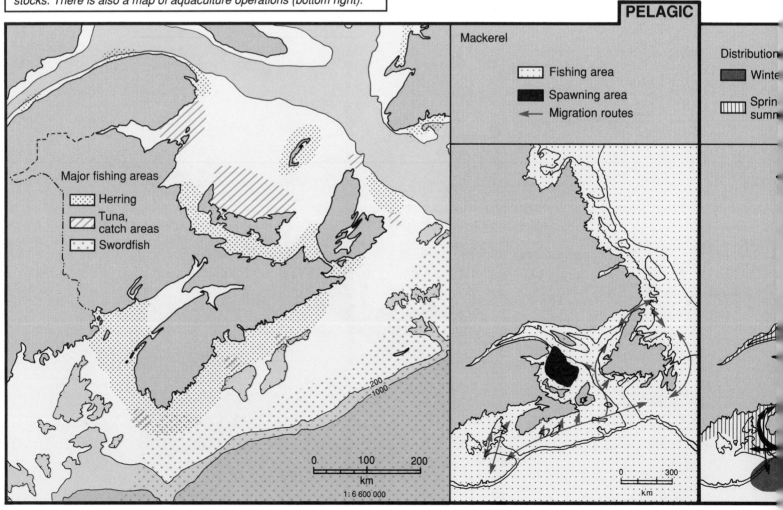

Major fishing areas

- Herring
- Tuna, catch areas
- Swordfish

0   100   200
km
1: 6 600 000

Mackerel

- Fishing area
- Spawning area
- Migration routes

Distribution

- Winter
- Spring summer

0   300
km

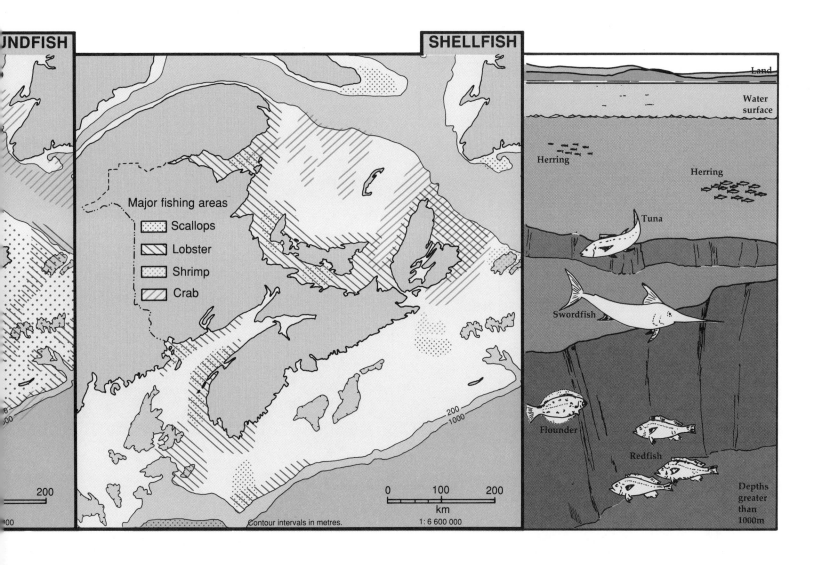

UNDFISH

SHELLFISH

Major fishing areas

- Scallops
- Lobster
- Shrimp
- Crab

200

200
1000

0   100   200
km

Contour intervals in metres.   1: 6 600 000

Land
Water surface
Herring
Herring
Tuna
Swordfish
Flounder
Redfish
Depths greater than 1000m

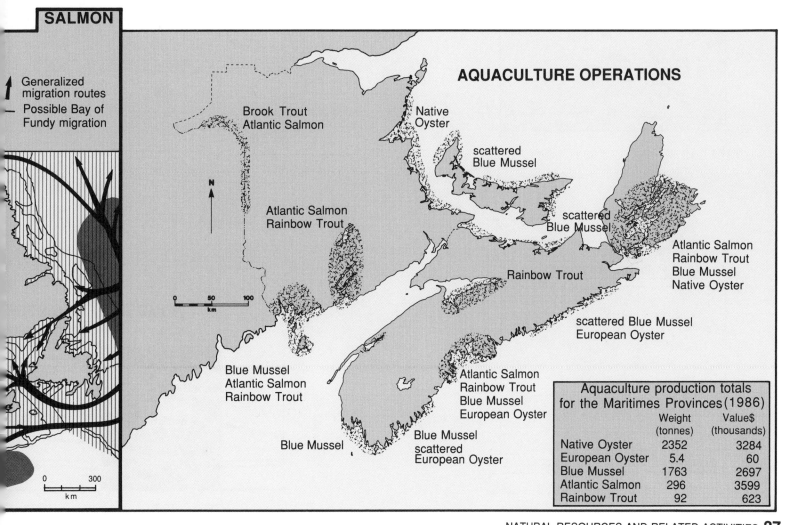

SALMON

Generalized migration routes
Possible Bay of Fundy migration

N

0   50   100
km

0   300
km

AQUACULTURE OPERATIONS

Brook Trout
Atlantic Salmon

Native Oyster

scattered Blue Mussel

Atlantic Salmon
Rainbow Trout

scattered Blue Mussel

Atlantic Salmon
Rainbow Trout
Blue Mussel
Native Oyster

Rainbow Trout

scattered Blue Mussel
European Oyster

Blue Mussel
Atlantic Salmon
Rainbow Trout

Atlantic Salmon
Rainbow Trout
Blue Mussel
European Oyster

Blue Mussel

Blue Mussel
scattered
European Oyster

Aquaculture production totals for the Maritimes Provinces (1986)		
	Weight (tonnes)	Value$ (thousands)
Native Oyster	2352	3284
European Oyster	5.4	60
Blue Mussel	1763	2697
Atlantic Salmon	296	3599
Rainbow Trout	92	623

FISH LANDINGS PLATE 13

The main map shows the number of fishermen and boats in the
Maritimes and indicates the landings by pie graphs. Value of
landings (below), licences for sport fishing (right) and changes in the
number of fishermen and boats(bottom) are shown in line graphs.

VALUE OF FISH LANDINGS

Groundfish
Shellfish

$ (millions)

175
150
125
100
75
50
25
0

N.S.
N.S.
N.B.
P.E.I.
N.B.
P.E.I.

1975 1977 1979 1981 1983 1985

N

0   50   100
km
1:2 800 000

Marine plants
Pelagic and estuarine

$ (millions)

30
20
10

N.S.
N.B.
P.E.I.
N.S.
N.B.

P.E.I.

1975 1977 1979 1981 1983 1985

Blanks indicate insufficient data.

NUMBER OF REGISTER

Numb
Numb

thousands

15
10
5
0

Not
available

1975 1976 1977 1978 1979

Map values:
196/76, 933/277, 1050/293, 594/146, 219/97, 264/87, 471/150, 102/40, 508/151, 601/211, 448/165, 337/122, 412/117, 301/117, 42/31, 37/27, 50/14, 15/12, 39/27, 161/76, 154/90, 207/67, 96/55, 68/39, 365/211, 41/29, 386/164, 88/71, 161/130, 336/105, 384/172, 403/106, 594/205, 821/267, 282/137, 578/282, 909/512, 1278/617

28 THE MARITIME PROVINCES ATLAS

LANDINGS BY TYPE BY FISHERIES STATISTICAL AREA, AND NUMBER OF FISHERMEN AND VESSELS BY FISHERIES STATISTICAL DISTRICT (1986)

ANGLING LICENCES FOR RECREATIONAL FISHING

RESIDENT

Landings by type

Groundfish

Shellfish

Pelagic and estuarine

| 152 | Number of fishermen |
| 67 | Number of vessels |

Value of landings ($ thousands)

- 100 000
- 50 000
- 30 000
- 15 000
- 6 000

HERMEN AND VESSELS

ered fishing vessels
ered fishermen

N.S.

N.B.
N.S.
P.E.I.
N.B.
P.E.I.

1981   1982   1983   1984   1985

NON-RESIDENT

N.B.

N.S.

P.E.I.

FISH PROCESSING PLATE 14

DISTRIBUTION OF FISH PROCESSING PLANTS BY TYPE AND NUMBER OF EMPLOYEES (1985)

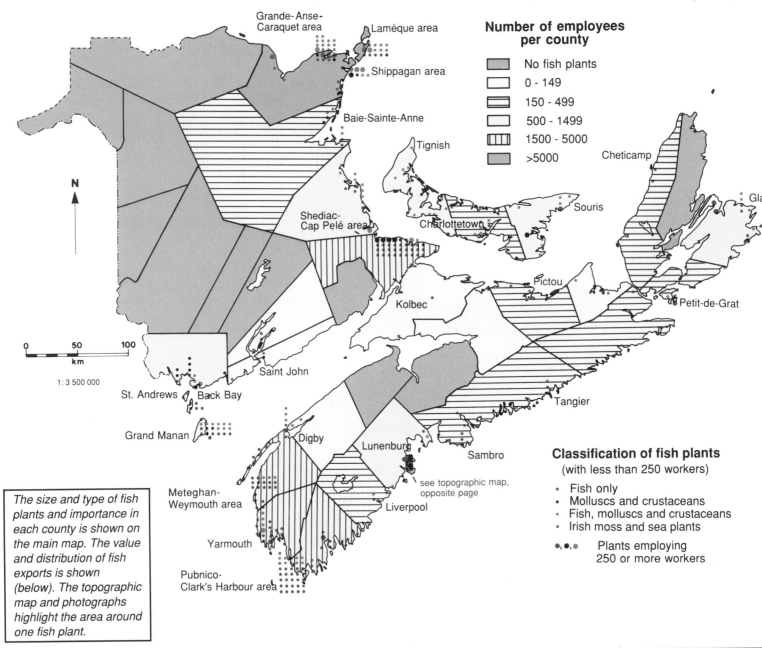

Number of employees per county

- No fish plants
- 0 - 149
- 150 - 499
- 500 - 1499
- 1500 - 5000
- >5000

Classification of fish plants
(with less than 250 workers)

- Fish only
- Molluscs and crustaceans
- Fish, molluscs and crustaceans
- Irish moss and sea plants

●,●,● Plants employing 250 or more workers

Grande-Anse-Caraquet area
Lamèque area
Shippagan area
Baie-Sainte-Anne
Tignish
Cheticamp
Glace
Souris
Shediac-Cap Pelé area
Charlottetown
Pictou
Petit-de-Grat
Kolbec
Saint John
St. Andrews Back Bay
Tangier
Grand Manan
Digby
Lunenburg
Sambro
Meteghan-Weymouth area
see topographic map, opposite page
Liverpool
Yarmouth
Pubnico-Clark's Harbour area

N

0   50   100
km
1 : 3 500 000

The size and type of fish plants and importance in each county is shown on the main map. The value and distribution of fish exports is shown (below). The topographic map and photographs highlight the area around one fish plant.

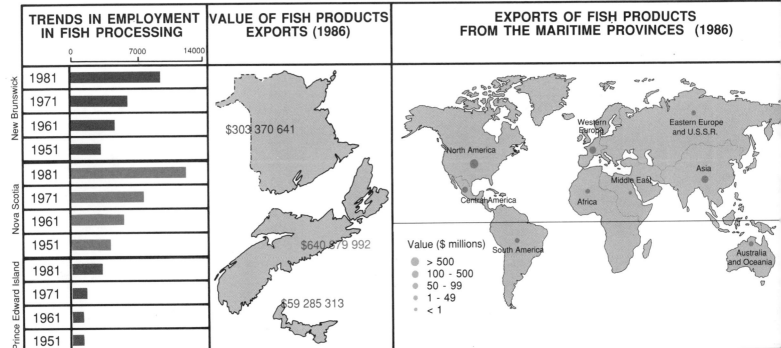

TRENDS IN EMPLOYMENT IN FISH PROCESSING

0   7000   14000

New Brunswick
1981
1971
1961
1951

Nova Scotia
1981
1971
1961
1951

Prince Edward Island
1981
1971
1961
1951

VALUE OF FISH PRODUCTS EXPORTS (1986)

$303 370 641

$640 879 992

$59 285 313

EXPORTS OF FISH PRODUCTS FROM THE MARITIME PROVINCES (1986)

Western Europe
Eastern Europe and U.S.S.R.
North America
Asia
Middle East
Central America
Africa
South America
Australia and Oceania

Value ($ millions)
- ● > 500
- ● 100 - 500
- ● 50 - 99
- ● 1 - 49
- ● < 1

anging land use with the construction of National Sea Products fish plant at Battery Point
ened: June 24, 1964 Employment, 1986: 1200 Fish processed, 1986: 36 500 tonnes

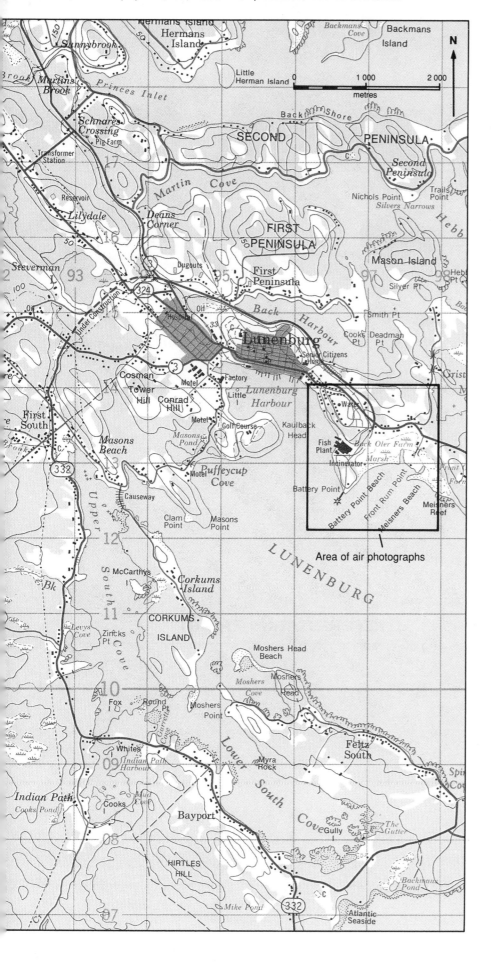

Area of air photographs

1958 Air photograph 1:21 120

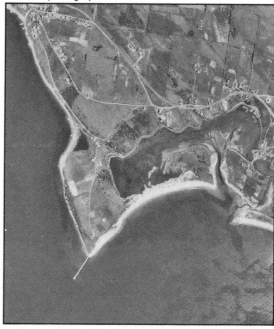

1986 Air photograph 1:21 276

1986 Oblique photograph looking west

FOREST RESOURCES PLATE 15

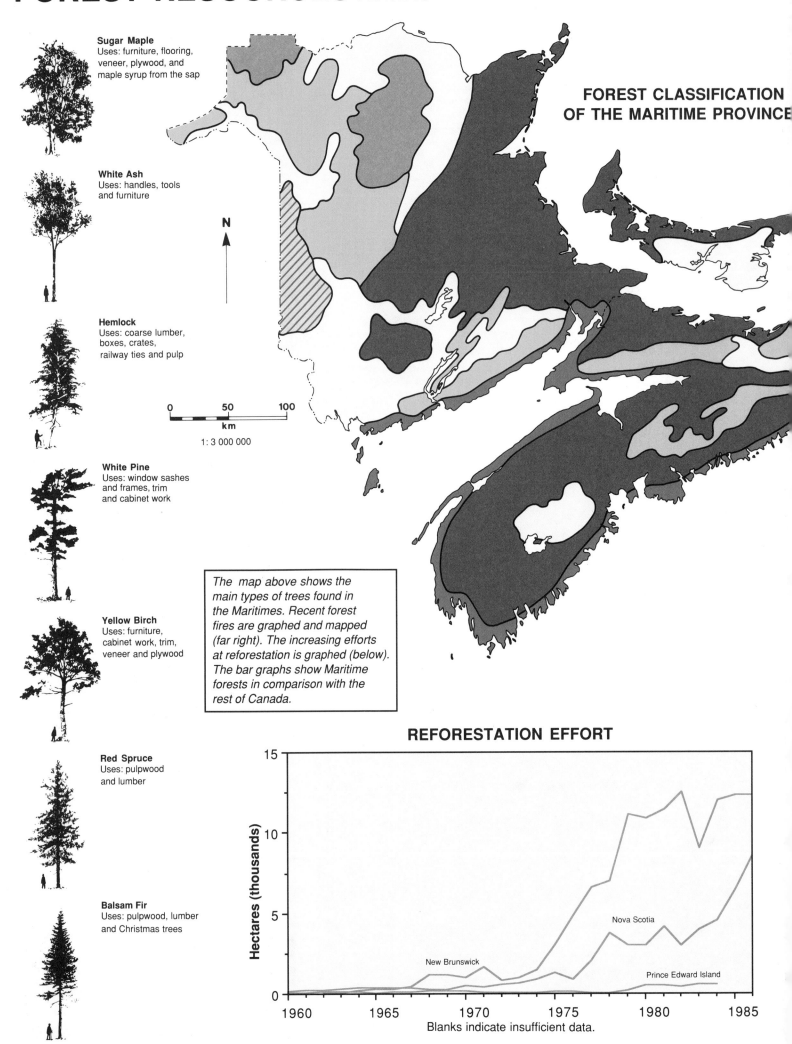

Sugar Maple
Uses: furniture, flooring, veneer, plywood, and maple syrup from the sap

White Ash
Uses: handles, tools and furniture

Hemlock
Uses: coarse lumber, boxes, crates, railway ties and pulp

White Pine
Uses: window sashes and frames, trim and cabinet work

Yellow Birch
Uses: furniture, cabinet work, trim, veneer and plywood

Red Spruce
Uses: pulpwood and lumber

Balsam Fir
Uses: pulpwood, lumber and Christmas trees

N

0   50   100
km
1: 3 000 000

FOREST CLASSIFICATION OF THE MARITIME PROVINCE

The map above shows the main types of trees found in the Maritimes. Recent forest fires are graphed and mapped (far right). The increasing efforts at reforestation is graphed (below). The bar graphs show Maritime forests in comparison with the rest of Canada.

REFORESTATION EFFORT

Hectares (thousands)

15

10

5

0

New Brunswick

Nova Scotia

Prince Edward Island

1960   1965   1970   1975   1980   1985

Blanks indicate insufficient data.

FOREST FIRES

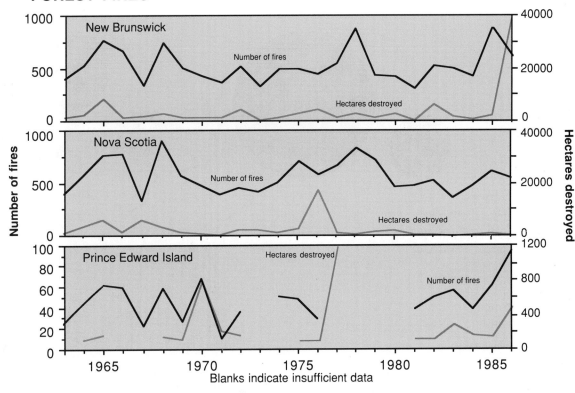

New Brunswick
Number of fires
Hectares destroyed

Nova Scotia
Number of fires
Hectares destroyed

Prince Edward Island
Hectares destroyed
Number of fires

Number of fires

Hectares destroyed

1965   1970   1975   1980   1985

Blanks indicate insufficient data

MAJOR FOREST FIRES, 1960 - 1986
(over 1000 hectares burned)

redominant tree species

- Sugar Maple-Ash
- Sugar Maple-Hemlock-Pine
- Sugar Maple-Yellow Birch-Pine
- Red Spruce-Hemlock-Pine
- Spruce-Fir
- Fir-Pine-Birch

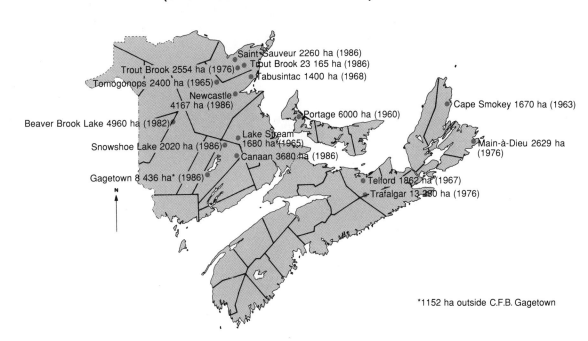

Saint-Sauveur 2260 ha (1986)
Trout Brook 23 165 ha (1986)
Trout Brook 2554 ha (1976)
Tabusintac 1400 ha (1968)
Tomogonops 2400 ha (1965)
Newcastle 4167 ha (1986)
Cape Smokey 1670 ha (1963)
Beaver Brook Lake 4960 ha (1982)
Portage 6000 ha (1960)
Lake Stream 1680 ha (1965)
Snowshoe Lake 2020 ha (1986)
Main-à-Dieu 2629 ha (1976)
Canaan 3680 ha (1986)
Gagetown 8 436 ha* (1986)
Telford 1862 ha (1967)
Trafalgar 13 280 ha (1976)

*1152 ha outside C.F.B. Gagetown

FOREST BIOMASS BY TYPE

CANADIAN REGIONS

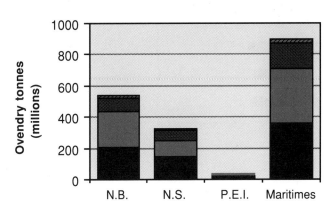

kon & N.W.T.
Atlantic
Quebec
Ontario
Prairies
ish Columbia

- Soft
- Mixed
- Hard
- Undetermined

0   2000   4000   6000   8000   10000
Ovendry tonnes (millions)

MARITIME PROVINCES

Ovendry tonnes (millions)

1000
800
600
400
200
0

N.B.   N.S.   P.E.I.   Maritimes

FOREST PRODUCTION AND WOOD PROCESSING

PLATE 16

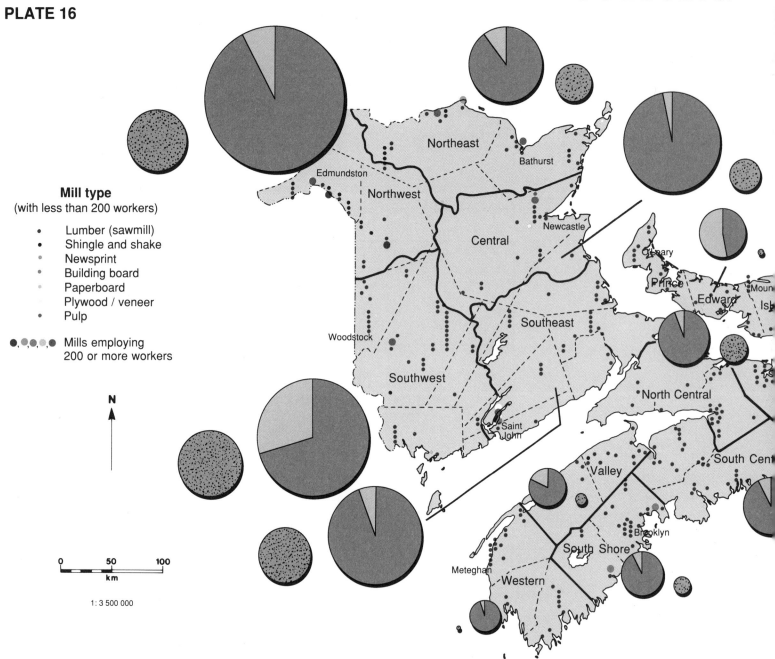

Mill type
(with less than 200 workers)

- Lumber (sawmill)
- Shingle and shake
- Newsprint
- Building board
- Paperboard
- Plywood / veneer
- Pulp

●,●,●,● Mills employing
200 or more workers

N

0   50   100
km

1 : 3 500 000

Edmundston
Northeast
Bathurst
Northwest
Central
Newcastle
Southeast
Woodstock
Southwest
Saint John
Calgary
Prince Edward Isl
Mount
North Central
Valley
South Cent
Brooklyn
South Shore
Meteghan
Western

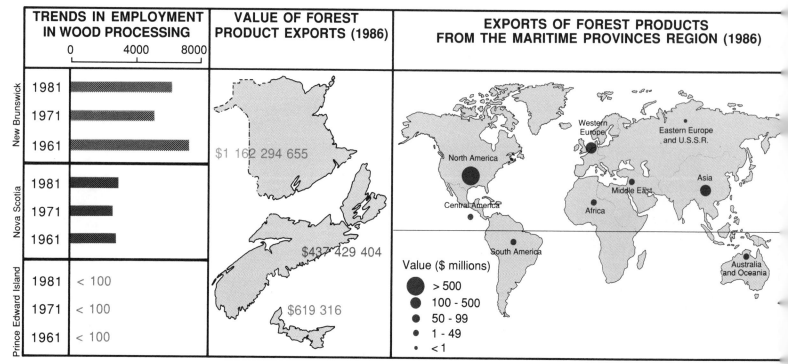

| TRENDS IN EMPLOYMENT IN WOOD PROCESSING | | VALUE OF FOREST PRODUCT EXPORTS (1986) | EXPORTS OF FOREST PRODUCTS FROM THE MARITIME PROVINCES REGION (1986) |

TRENDS IN EMPLOYMENT IN WOOD PROCESSING

0   4000   8000

New Brunswick
1981
1971
1961

Nova Scotia
1981
1971
1961

Prince Edward Island
1981 < 100
1971 < 100
1961 < 100

VALUE OF FOREST PRODUCT EXPORTS (1986)

$1 162 294 655

$437 429 404

$619 316

EXPORTS OF FOREST PRODUCTS FROM THE MARITIME PROVINCES REGION (1986)

Western Europe
Eastern Europe and U.S.S.R.
North America
Asia
Middle East
Central America
Africa
South America
Australia and Oceania

Value ($ millions)
- > 500
- 100 - 500
- 50 - 99
- 1 - 49
- < 1

The map shows the amount of forest production and the location of mills. On the right is a table listing other types of wood processors. The value and distribution of exported forest products is shown (bottom). The bar graphs compare Maritime wood production with that of other Canadian regions.

FOREST PRODUCTION (m³) BY REGION AND WOOD PRODUCT MILLS (1985-1986)

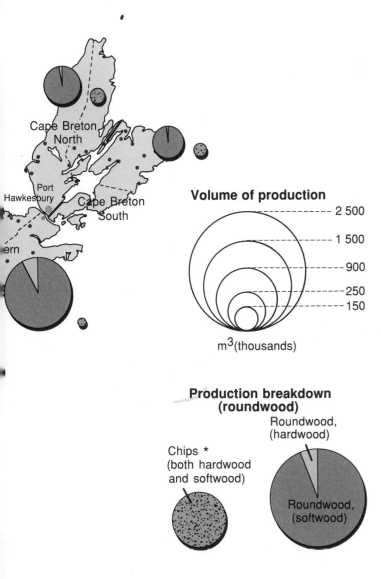

Cape Breton North

Port Hawkesbury

Cape Breton South

ern

Volume of production

— 2 500
— 1 500
— 900
— 250
— 150

m³(thousands)

Production breakdown (roundwood)

Chips * (both hardwood and softwood)

Roundwood, (hardwood)

Roundwood, (softwood)

Chips may be by-products of sawmills or produced from whole trees.

	Prefabricated wooden buildings	Kitchen cabinets and vanities	Doors and windows	Boxes and pallets	Coffins and caskets	Wood preservation and treating	Fences, barrels, stairs and trusses	Wooden household furniture
N. B.								
Albert								
Carleton	2	2	3	1			10	2
Charlotte	1	2					10	
Gloucester	2	4	9	2			11	2
Kent	2	4	3	1		1	2	
Kings	2	5	1			4	6	
Madawaska	2	2	1		1		4	1
Northumberland	2	4	4	2		1	6	2
Queens		2		1			3	1
Restigouche	2	2	4	2		1	6	2
St. John		7	4	4	1		10	3
Sunbury		1					1	
Victoria	1	2	2	1			5	2
Westmorland	6	10	9	4	1		14	4
York	4	5	3			1	3	11
N. S.								
Annapolis		3	1				3	
Antigonish							2	
Cape Breton	3	2	2				5	2
Colchester	3	3	3			2	8	4
Cumberland		2	4				1	1
Digby	2		3	1	1		2	2
Guysborough				1				1
Halifax	3	16	9	1			8	7
Hants		2		1		1	1	1
Inverness		1	2				1	2
Kings		2	1	1			3	2
Lunenburg		2	2	5			11	3
Pictou		4	1			1	7	2
Queens							2	1
Richmond								1
Shelburne			1				2	2
Victoria							2	
Yarmouth			2	1			5	1
P.E.I.								
Kings	1		2	1				2
Prince			4	7				8
Queens	1	2	12	5			1	9

WOOD PRODUCTION (1984)

CANADIAN REGIONS

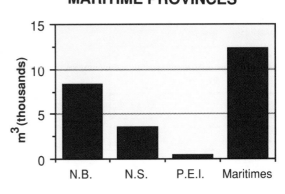

Atlantic

Quebec

Ontario

Prairies

tish Columbia

0   20   40   60   80

m³(thousands)

MARITIME PROVINCES

15

m³ (thousands)

10

5

0

N.B.   N.S.   P.E.I.   Maritimes

QUARRYING AND MINING OPERATIONS AND VALUE OF PRODUCTION (1985)

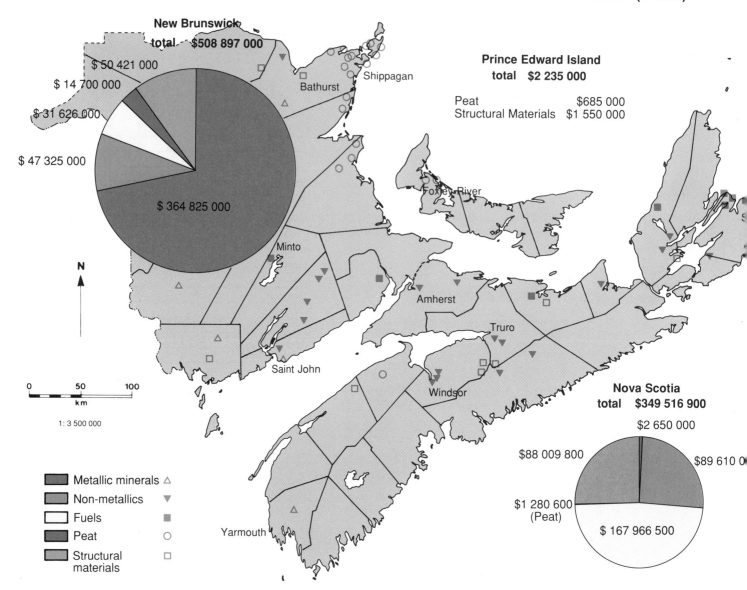

New Brunswick
total   **$508 897 000**

$ 50 421 000
$ 14 700 000
$ 31 626 000
$ 47 325 000
$ 364 825 000

Shippagan
Bathurst
Minto
Saint John
Yarmouth

Prince Edward Island
total   **$2 235 000**

Peat $685 000
Structural Materials $1 550 000

Foxley River
Amherst
Truro
Windsor

Nova Scotia
total   **$349 516 900**

$2 650 000
$88 009 800
$89 610 0
$1 280 600
(Peat)
$ 167 966 500

N

0   50   100
km
1 : 3 500 000

Legend	
Metallic minerals	△
Non-metallics	▼
Fuels	■
Peat	○
Structural materials	□

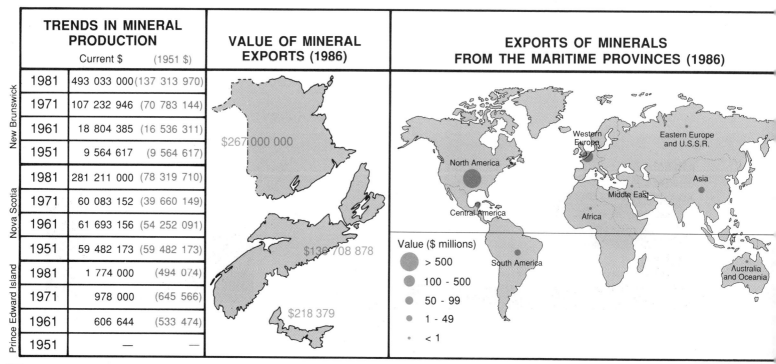

TRENDS IN MINERAL PRODUCTION

		Current $	(1951 $)
New Brunswick	1981	493 033 000	(137 313 970)
	1971	107 232 946	(70 783 144)
	1961	18 804 385	(16 536 311)
	1951	9 564 617	(9 564 617)
Nova Scotia	1981	281 211 000	(78 319 710)
	1971	60 083 152	(39 660 149)
	1961	61 693 156	(54 252 091)
	1951	59 482 173	(59 482 173)
Prince Edward Island	1981	1 774 000	(494 074)
	1971	978 000	(645 566)
	1961	606 644	(533 474)
	1951	—	—

VALUE OF MINERAL EXPORTS (1986)

$267 000 000
$136 708 878
$218 379

EXPORTS OF MINERALS FROM THE MARITIME PROVINCES (1986)

Western Europe
Eastern Europe and U.S.S.R.
North America
Asia
Middle East
Central America
Africa
South America
Australia and Oceania

Value ($ millions)
> 500
100 - 500
50 - 99
1 - 49
< 1

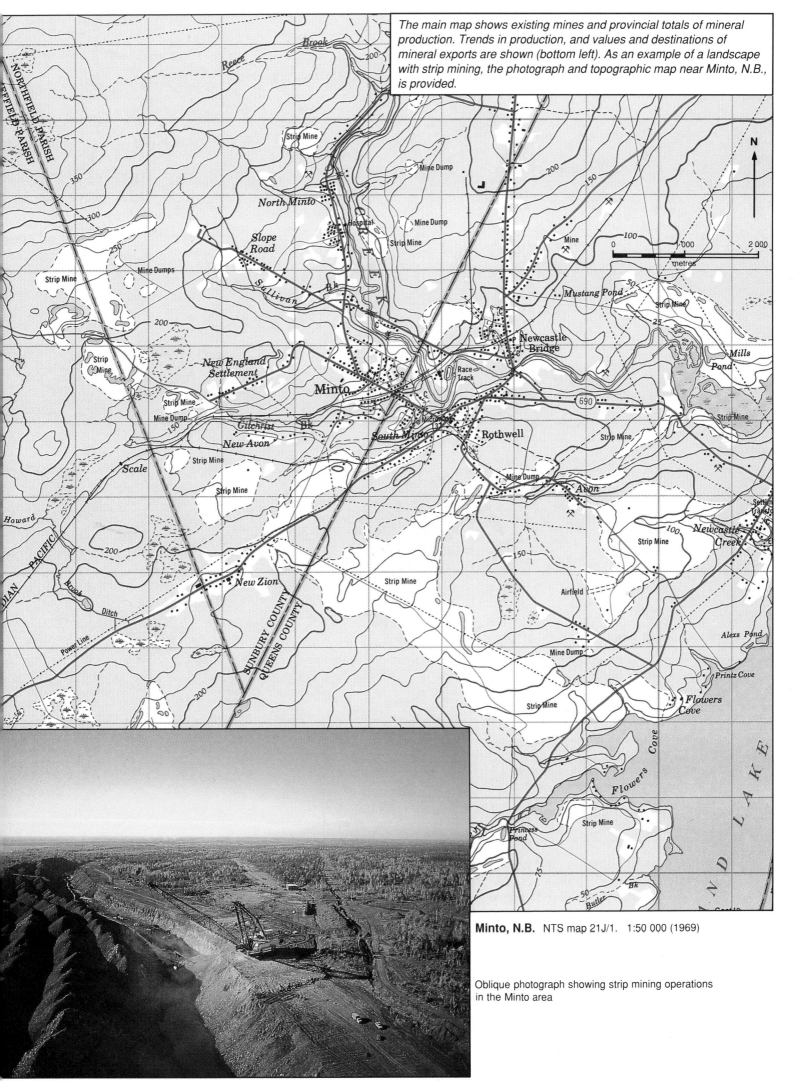

The main map shows existing mines and provincial totals of mineral production. Trends in production, and values and destinations of mineral exports are shown (bottom left). As an example of a landscape with strip mining, the photograph and topographic map near Minto, N.B., is provided.

N

0   1 000   2 000
metres

Minto, N.B. NTS map 21J/1. 1:50 000 (1969)

Oblique photograph showing strip mining operations in the Minto area

ELECTRICAL ENERGY PLATE 18

ELECTRICAL GENERATING PLANTS BY TYPE, LOCATION AND CAPACITY (1987)

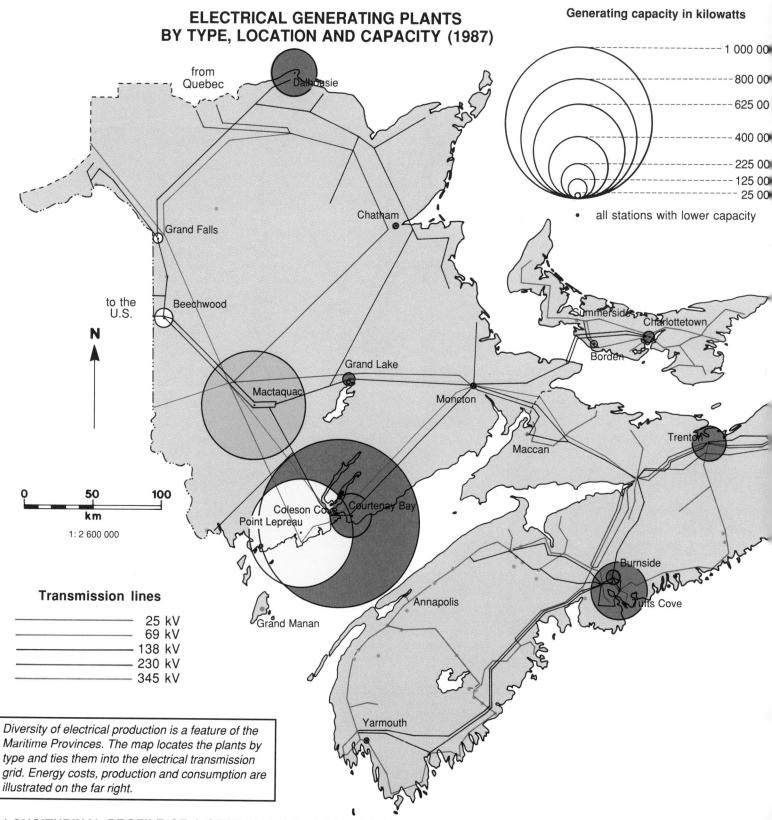

Generating capacity in kilowatts

- 1 000 00
- 800 00
- 625 00
- 400 00
- 225 00
- 125 00
- 25 00

• all stations with lower capacity

from Quebec

Dalhousie

Chatham

Grand Falls

to the U.S.

Beechwood

N

Grand Lake

Mactaquac

Moncton

Summerside

Charlottetown

Borden

Trenton

Maccan

Coleson Cove

Courtenay Bay

Point Lepreau

Burnside

Tufts Cove

Annapolis

Grand Manan

Yarmouth

0   50   100
km
1: 2 600 000

Transmission lines

————————	25 kV
————————	69 kV
————————	138 kV
————————	230 kV
————————	345 kV

Diversity of electrical production is a feature of the Maritime Provinces. The map locates the plants by type and ties them into the electrical transmission grid. Energy costs, production and consumption are illustrated on the far right.

LONGITUDINAL PROFILE OF A SECTION OF THE SAINT JOHN RIVER SHOWING SITES OF HYDRO-ELECTRICITY GENERATION
(elevations are above sea level)

Grand Falls
4 units
63 mW capacity
130.2m
90.3m

Beechwood
3 units
115 mW capacity
74.1m
57.3m

Mactaquac
6 units
653 mW capacity
40.5m
5.6m

metres: 160 140 120 100 80 60 40 20 0

horizontal scale 1:2 666 666
vertical scale 1:5333
vertical exaggeration 500

Edmundston

Fredericton

— 252 kilometres via the river —

ELECTRICIT

Province	Hydro	Wind, Tidal	Stear
New Brunswick	3 121 271		4 263
Nova Scotia	1 034 714	8 340	6 192
Prince Edward Island			1 42

1 megawatt=1000 kilowatts
kW.h - kilowatt hour
mW.h - megawatt hour
kV - kilovolts

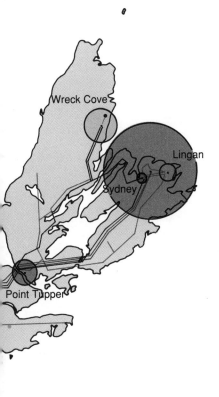

Type of plant

○ Nuclear ◐ Hydro

◑ Oil/coal ● Tidal

◔ Diesel ● Gas turbine

● Wind turbine

UCTION mW.h (1984)

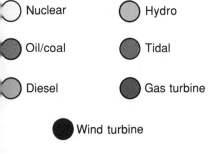

	Thermal		Total Thermal	Total
ustion	Nuclear	Gas Turbine		
4	5 011 393		9 274 680	12 395 951
		186	6 192 823	7 235 877
5		275	2 138	2 138

CANADIAN ELECTRICAL ENERGY COSTS   JANUARY 1,1987
($ per 5 000 kW.h)

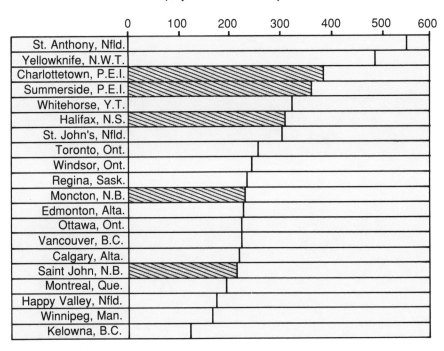

ELECTRICAL PRODUCTION, CONSUMPTION AND MOVEMENT (1984)

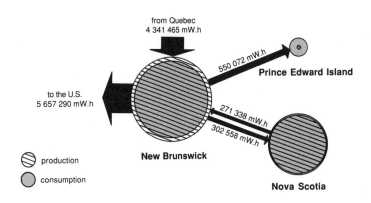

CHANGES IN ELECTRICAL PRODUCTION SINCE 1956

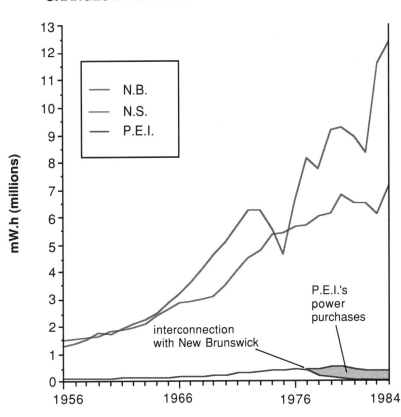

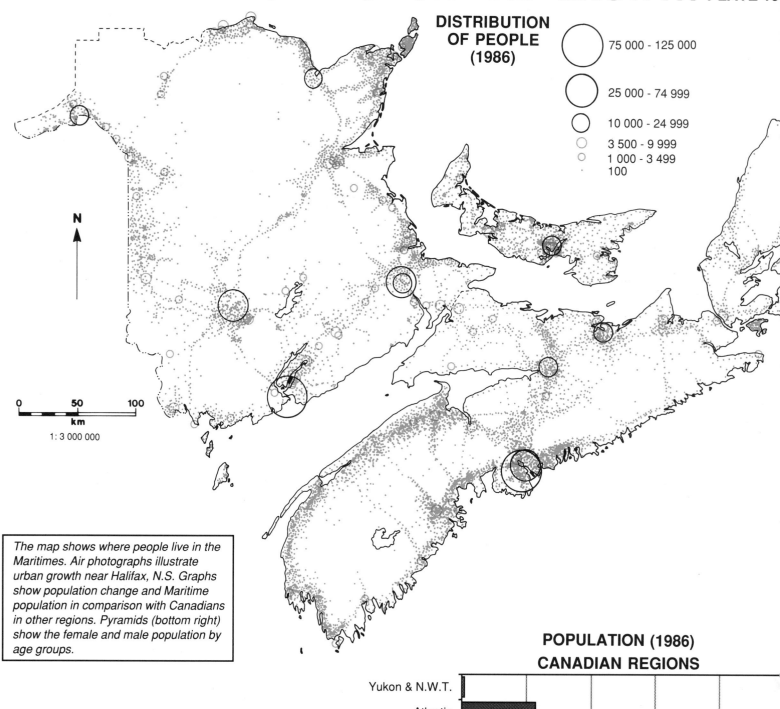

DISTRIBUTION
OF PEOPLE
(1986)

75 000 - 125 000

25 000 - 74 999

10 000 - 24 999

3 500 - 9 999
1 000 - 3 499
100

N

| 0 | 50 | 100 |
km
1 : 3 000 000

The map shows where people live in the Maritimes. Air photographs illustrate urban growth near Halifax, N.S. Graphs show population change and Maritime population in comparison with Canadians in other regions. Pyramids (bottom right) show the female and male population by age groups.

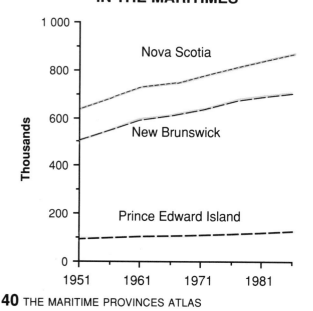

POPULATION GROWTH
IN THE MARITIMES

Nova Scotia

New Brunswick

Prince Edward Island

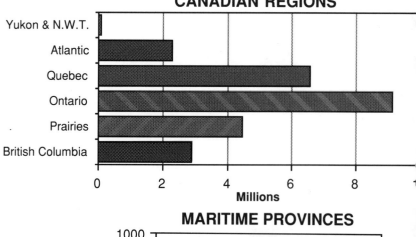

POPULATION (1986)
CANADIAN REGIONS

Yukon & N.W.T.
Atlantic
Quebec
Ontario
Prairies
British Columbia

Millions

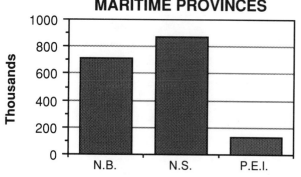

MARITIME PROVINCES

N.B.   N.S.   P.E.I.

URBAN GROWTH AT CLAYTON PARK, HALIFAX, N.S.

N

0 50 100
metres
1:10 000

1 Bayview Road	5 Lacewood Drive
2 Bedford Highway	6 Mount St. Vincent University
3 Clayton Park Drive	7 Elementary School
4 Dunbrack Street	8 Junior High School

1966   **1982**

POPULATION PYRAMIDS FOR THE MARITIME PROVINCES

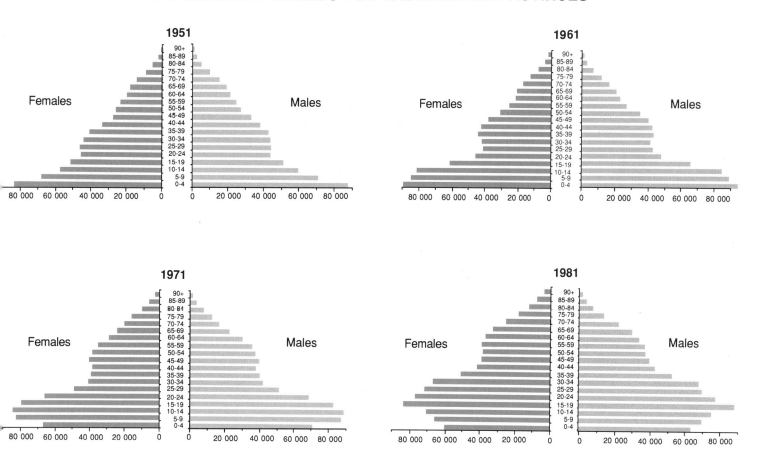

URBAN-RURAL AND NATIVE POPULATION, AND ETHNIC ORIGIN PLATE 20

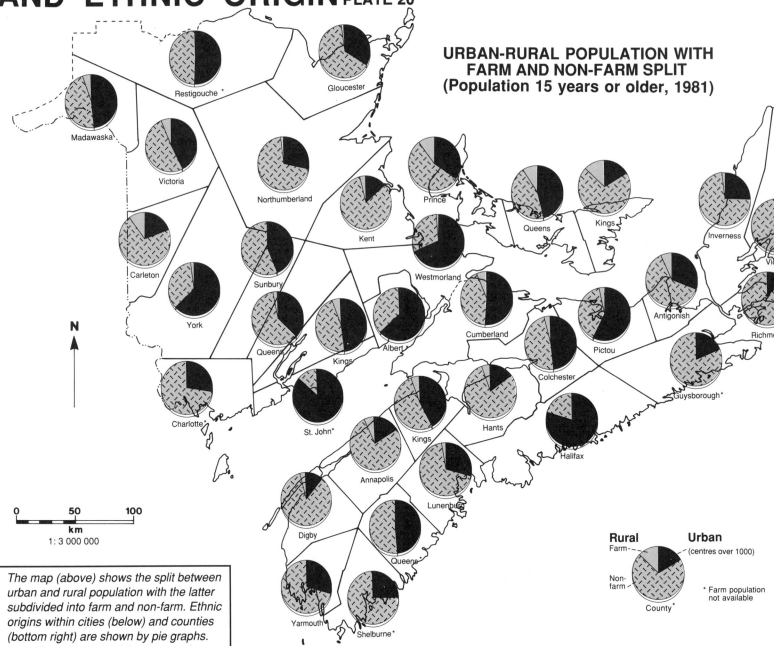

URBAN-RURAL POPULATION WITH FARM AND NON-FARM SPLIT
(Population 15 years or older, 1981)

Rural   **Urban**
Farm —   (centres over 1000)

Non-farm —

County *

* Farm population not available

The map (above) shows the split between urban and rural population with the latter subdivided into farm and non-farm. Ethnic origins within cities (below) and counties (bottom right) are shown by pie graphs. The map (upper right) focuses on the distribution of Natives living on reserves.

ETHNIC ORIGIN FOR SELECTED URBAN CENTRES (1981)

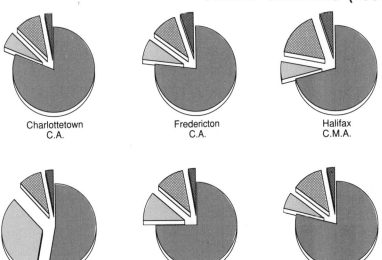

Charlottetown C.A.

Fredericton C.A.

Halifax C.M.A.

Moncton C.A.

Saint John C.M.A.

Sydney C.A.

All other

Other European

French

British

C.A. - Census Agglomeration
C.M.A.- Census Metropolitan Area

INDIAN RESERVES BY CENSUS POPULATION* (1986)

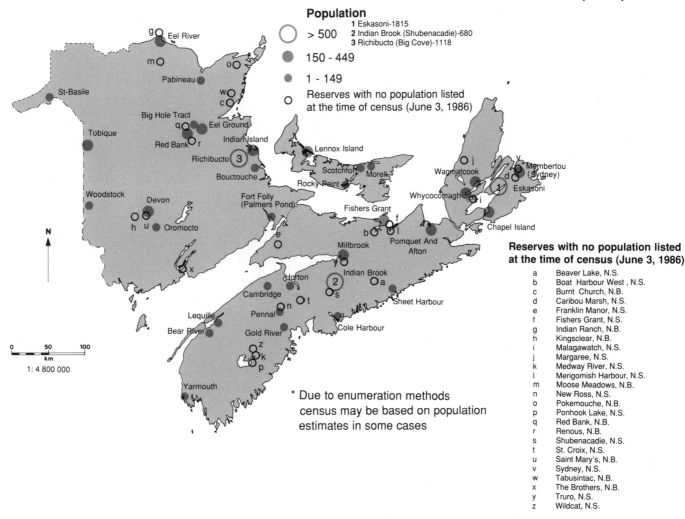

Population

○	> 500	**1** Eskasoni-1815
		2 Indian Brook (Shubenacadie)-680
		3 Richibucto (Big Cove)-1118
●	150 - 449	
●	1 - 149	
○	Reserves with no population listed at the time of census (June 3, 1986)	

Reserves with no population listed at the time of census (June 3, 1986)

a	Beaver Lake, N.S.
b	Boat Harbour West , N.S.
c	Burnt Church, N.B.
d	Caribou Marsh, N.S.
e	Franklin Manor, N.S.
f	Fishers Grant, N.S.
g	Indian Ranch, N.B.
h	Kingsclear, N.B.
i	Malagawatch, N.S.
j	Margaree, N.S.
k	Medway River, N.S.
l	Merigomish Harbour, N.S.
m	Moose Meadows, N.B.
n	New Ross, N.S.
o	Pokemouche, N.B.
p	Ponhook Lake, N.S.
q	Red Bank, N.B.
r	Renous, N.B.
s	Shubenacadie, N.S.
t	St. Croix, N.S.
u	Saint Mary's, N.B.
v	Sydney, N.S.
w	Tabusintac, N.B.
x	The Brothers, N.B.
y	Truro, N.S.
z	Wildcat, N.S.

* Due to enumeration methods census may be based on population estimates in some cases

ETHNIC ORIGIN FOR COUNTIES (1981)

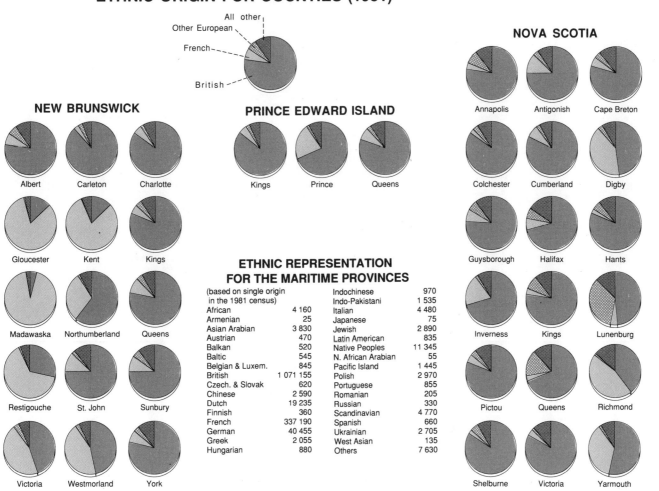

NEW BRUNSWICK

Albert, Carleton, Charlotte

Gloucester, Kent, Kings

Madawaska, Northumberland, Queens

Restigouche, St. John, Sunbury

Victoria, Westmorland, York

PRINCE EDWARD ISLAND

Kings, Prince, Queens

NOVA SCOTIA

Annapolis, Antigonish, Cape Breton

Colchester, Cumberland, Digby

Guysborough, Halifax, Hants

Inverness, Kings, Lunenburg

Pictou, Queens, Richmond

Shelburne, Victoria, Yarmouth

ETHNIC REPRESENTATION FOR THE MARITIME PROVINCES

(based on single origin in the 1981 census)

African	4 160	Indochinese	970
Armenian	25	Indo-Pakistani	1 535
Asian Arabian	3 830	Italian	4 480
Austrian	470	Japanese	75
Balkan	520	Jewish	2 890
Baltic	545	Latin American	835
Belgian & Luxem.	845	Native Peoples	11 345
British	1 071 155	N. African Arabian	55
Czech. & Slovak	620	Pacific Island	1 445
Chinese	2 590	Polish	2 970
Dutch	19 235	Portuguese	855
Finnish	360	Romanian	205
French	337 190	Russian	330
German	40 455	Scandinavian	4 770
Greek	2 055	Spanish	660
Hungarian	880	Ukrainian	2 705
		West Asian	135
		Others	7 630

CITIES PLATE 21

URBAN LAND USE

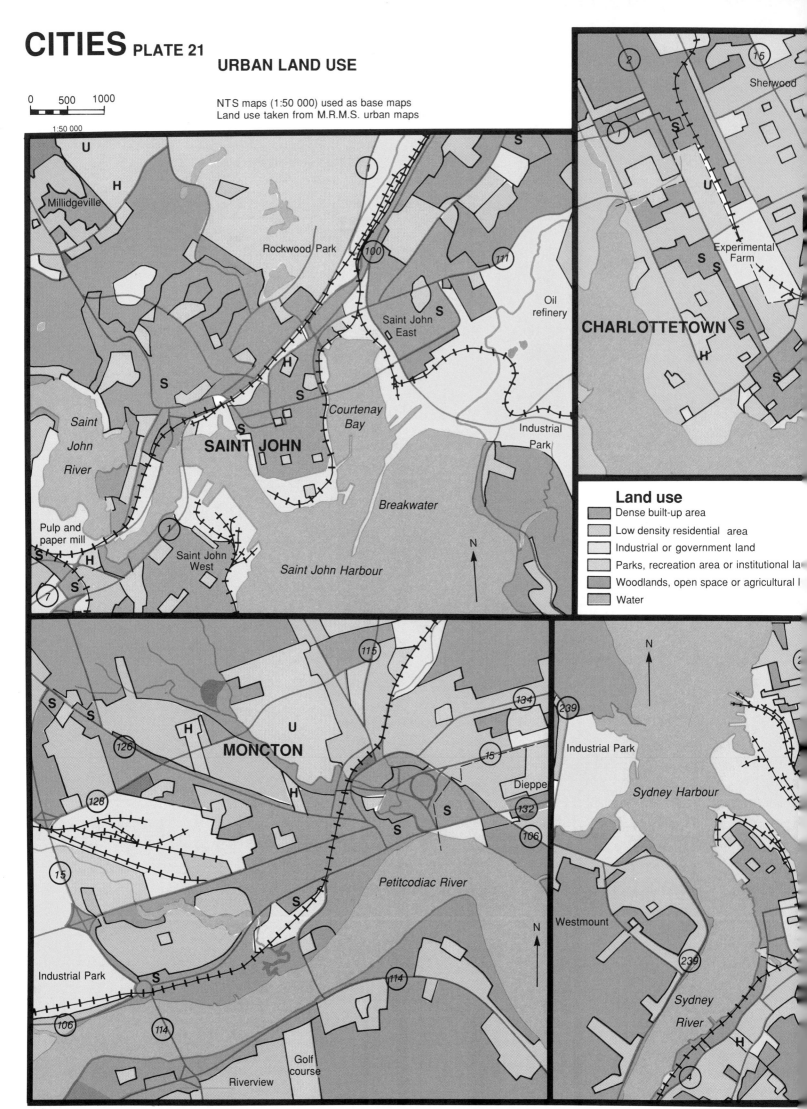

0   500   1000

1:50 000

NTS maps (1:50 000) used as base maps
Land use taken from M.R.M.S. urban maps

CHARLOTTETOWN

Sherwood

Experimental Farm

U

Millidgeville

H

Rockwood Park

Oil refinery

Saint John East

S

Industrial Park

SAINT JOHN

Courtenay Bay

Saint John River

Breakwater

N

Pulp and paper mill

Saint John West

Saint John Harbour

Land use

- Dense built-up area
- Low density residential area
- Industrial or government land
- Parks, recreation area or institutional la
- Woodlands, open space or agricultural l
- Water

MONCTON

U

H

H

S

S

Industrial Park

Dieppe

Sydney Harbour

S

Petitcodiac River

N

Westmount

Industrial Park

N

Sydney River

H

Golf course

Riverview

N

Bedford Basin

Industrial Park

Quarry

(118)

(111)

S

S

DARTMOUTH

S

Golf course

S

(7)

S

I

(2)

U

Clayton Park
air photograph
(see page 41)

S

S

S

Halifax Harbour

Ferry

Ferry

S

HALIFAX

S

S

H

S

S

S

H U

(102)

Golf course

S

S

H

H

H

U

H

(103)

(3)

U

6

H

Point Pleasant
Park

— — City boundary
H   Hospital
—   Main road
+   Railroad
S   Shopping centre
U   University

(2)

H

H

Industrial
Park

Hillsborough River

N

Southport

(1)

S

Nashwaaksis

S

S

(105)

S

Saint John River

Devon

(102)

N

Golf
course

S

SYDNEY

(4)

S

FREDERICTON

(125)

Odell Park
Game Refuge

(105)

(2)

U

S

S

(101)

H

S

(2)

Topographic map
at 1: 50 000
Charlottetown
11 L/3 and 11 L/6
Fredericton
21 G/15
Halifax/Dartmouth
11 D/12
Moncton
21 I/2
Saint John
21 G/8
Sydney
11 K/1

EDUCATION, FIRST LANGUAGE AND RELIGIOUS PREFERENCE PLATE 22

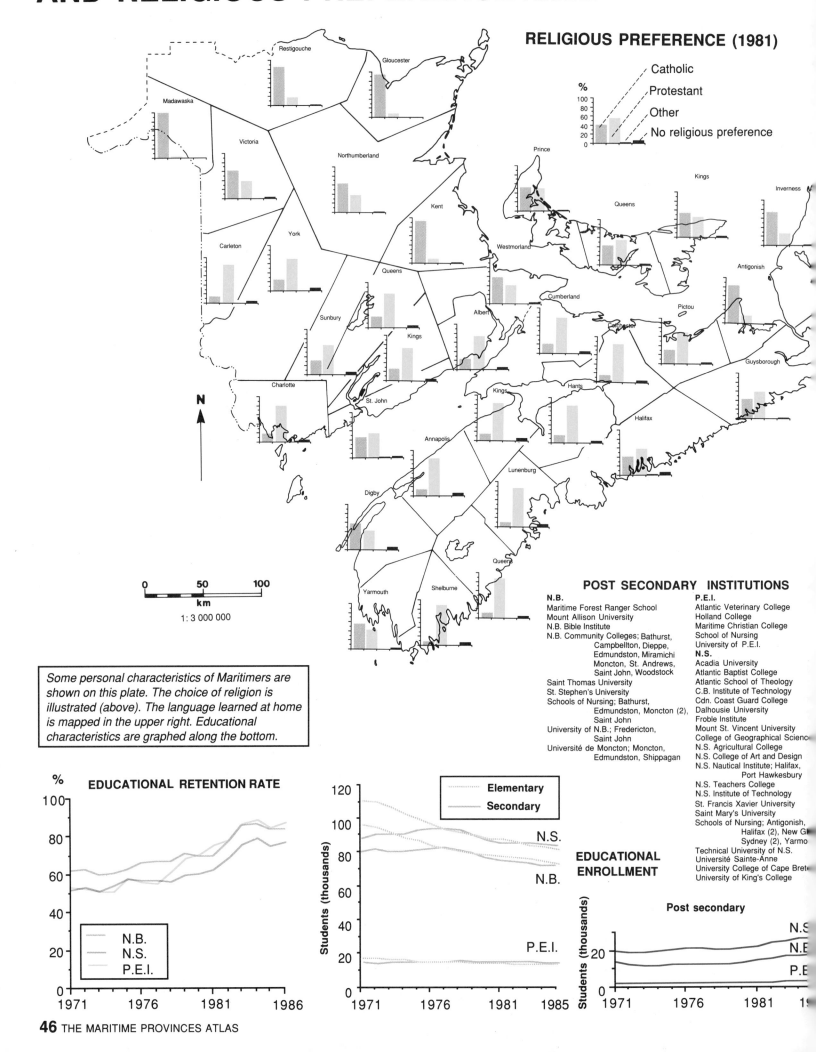

RELIGIOUS PREFERENCE (1981)

- - - - Catholic
- - - - Protestant
- - - - Other
- - - - No religious preference

Some personal characteristics of Maritimers are shown on this plate. The choice of religion is illustrated (above). The language learned at home is mapped in the upper right. Educational characteristics are graphed along the bottom.

1 : 3 000 000

POST SECONDARY INSTITUTIONS

N.B.
Maritime Forest Ranger School
Mount Allison University
N.B. Bible Institute
N.B. Community Colleges; Bathurst,
    Campbellton, Dieppe,
    Edmundston, Miramichi
    Moncton, St. Andrews,
    Saint John, Woodstock
Saint Thomas University
St. Stephen's University
Schools of Nursing; Bathurst,
    Edmundston, Moncton (2),
    Saint John
University of N.B.; Fredericton,
    Saint John
Université de Moncton; Moncton,
    Edmundston, Shippagan

P.E.I.
Atlantic Veterinary College
Holland College
Maritime Christian College
School of Nursing
University of P.E.I.
N.S.
Acadia University
Atlantic Baptist College
Atlantic School of Theology
C.B. Institute of Technology
Cdn. Coast Guard College
Dalhousie University
Froble Institute
Mount St. Vincent University
College of Geographical Science
N.S. Agricultural College
N.S. College of Art and Design
N.S. Nautical Institute; Halifax,
    Port Hawkesbury
N.S. Teachers College
N.S. Institute of Technology
St. Francis Xavier University
Saint Mary's University
Schools of Nursing; Antigonish,
    Halifax (2), New Gl
    Sydney (2), Yarmo
Technical University of N.S.
Université Sainte-Anne
University College of Cape Bret
University of King's College

EDUCATIONAL RETENTION RATE

%
100
80
60
40
20
0

N.B.
N.S.
P.E.I.

1971   1976   1981   1986

Elementary
Secondary

120
100
80
60
40
20

N.S.
N.B.
P.E.I.

1971   1976   1981   1985

Students (thousands)

EDUCATIONAL ENROLLMENT

Post secondary

N.S
N.B
P.E.I

20

Students (thousands)

1971   1976   1981

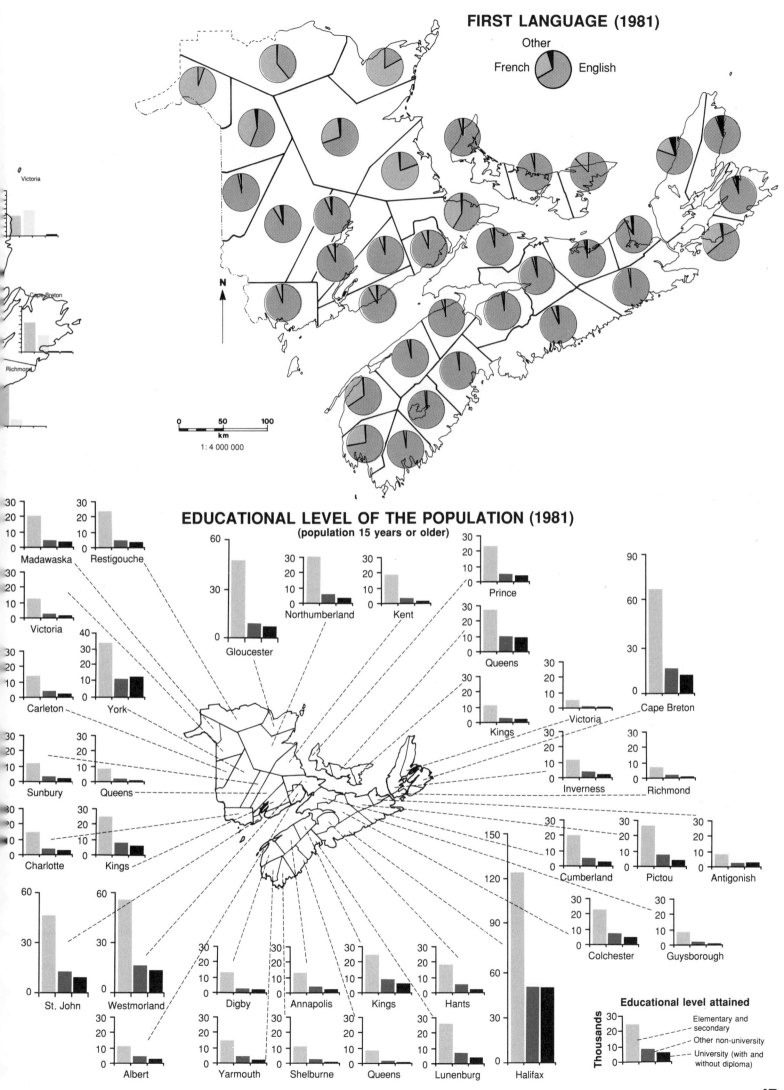

FIRST LANGUAGE (1981)

Other
French — English

EDUCATIONAL LEVEL OF THE POPULATION (1981)
(population 15 years or older)

Madawaska

Restigouche

Victoria

Carleton

York

Sunbury

Queens

Charlotte

Kings

St. John

Westmorland

Albert

Gloucester

Northumberland

Kent

Digby

Yarmouth

Annapolis

Shelburne

Kings

Queens

Hants

Lunenburg

Halifax

Prince

Queens

Kings

Victoria

Cape Breton

Inverness

Richmond

Cumberland

Pictou

Antigonish

Colchester

Guysborough

Educational level attained

Thousands

Elementary and secondary

Other non-university

University (with and without diploma)

Victoria

Cape Breton

Richmond

VITAL STATISTICS PLATE 23

BIRTHS (1985)

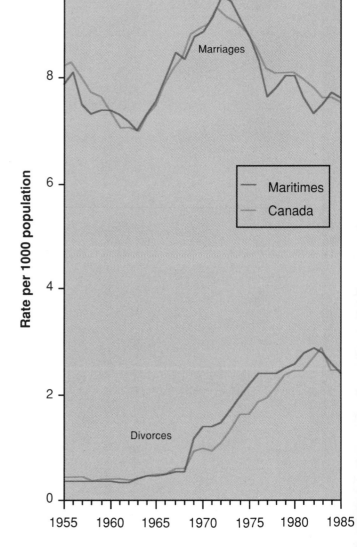

Average rates per 1000*
Maritime Provinces 14.2
Canada 15.4

Rate per 1000*
- > 19.0
- 16.0 - 19.0
- 13.0 - 15.9
- 10.0 - 12.9
- 5.0 - 9.9

BIRTH AND DEATH RATES (1955-1985)

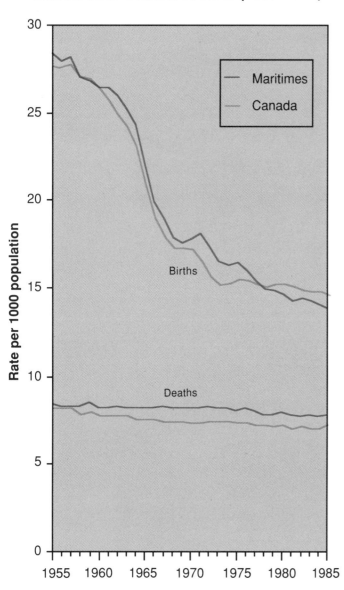

— Maritimes
— Canada

Births

Deaths

Rate per 1000 population

1955 1960 1965 1970 1975 1980 1985

MARRIAGE AND DIVORCE RATES (1955-1985)

Marriages

— Maritimes
— Canada

Divorces

Rate per 1000 population

1955 1960 1965 1970 1975 1980 1985

MARRIAGES (1985)

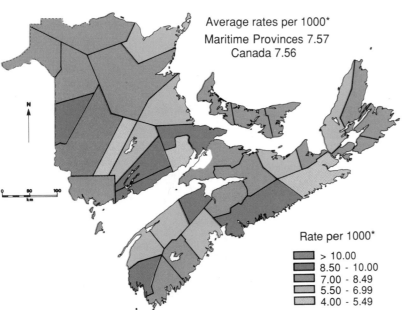

Average rates per 1000*
Maritime Provinces 7.57
Canada 7.56

Rate per 1000*
- > 10.00
- 8.50 - 10.00
- 7.00 - 8.49
- 5.50 - 6.99
- 4.00 - 5.49

* Based on 1981 populations

DEATHS DUE TO DISEASES OF THE CIRCULATORY SYSTEM (1985)

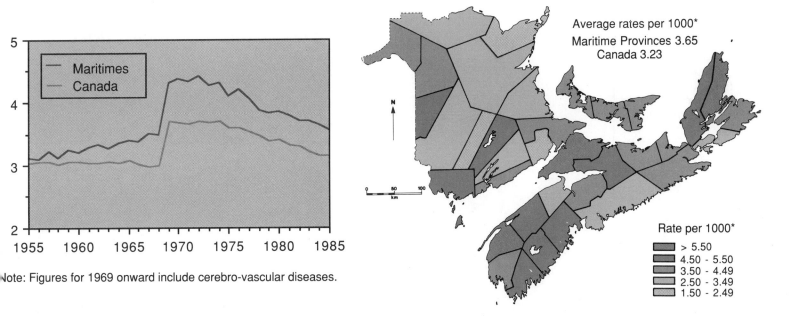

Note: Figures for 1969 onward include cerebro-vascular diseases.

Average rates per 1000*
Maritime Provinces 3.65
Canada 3.23

Rate per 1000*
> 5.50
4.50 - 5.50
3.50 - 4.49
2.50 - 3.49
1.50 - 2.49

DEATHS DUE TO CANCERS (1985)

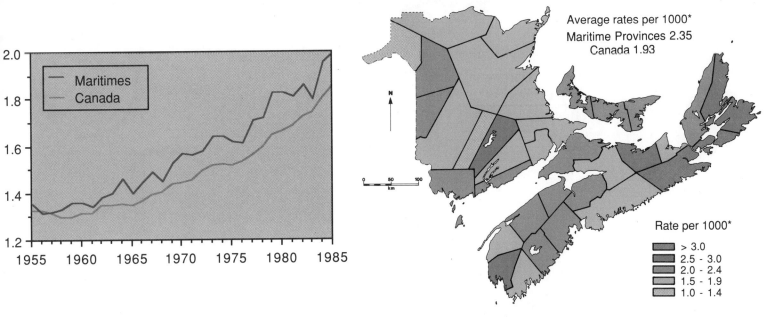

Average rates per 1000*
Maritime Provinces 2.35
Canada 1.93

Rate per 1000*
> 3.0
2.5 - 3.0
2.0 - 2.4
1.5 - 1.9
1.0 - 1.4

DEATHS DUE TO MOTOR VEHICLE ACCIDENTS (1985)

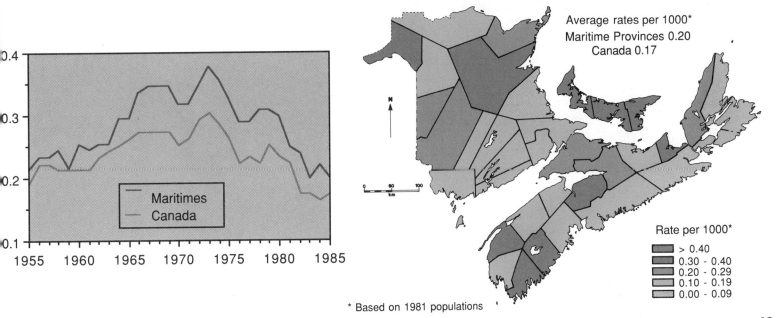

Average rates per 1000*
Maritime Provinces 0.20
Canada 0.17

Rate per 1000*
> 0.40
0.30 - 0.40
0.20 - 0.29
0.10 - 0.19
0.00 - 0.09

* Based on 1981 populations

INTERPROVINCIAL MIGRATION AND IMMIGRATION PLATE 24

People migrating to and from the Maritimes are shown on this page. The width of the lines indicates the number of migrants. The total effect of in- and out-migration for each province is graphed. People coming from other parts of the world to the Maritime Provinces are mapped in the lower right.

MARITIME PROVINCES IN-MIGRATION FROM OTHER CANADIAN PROVINCES

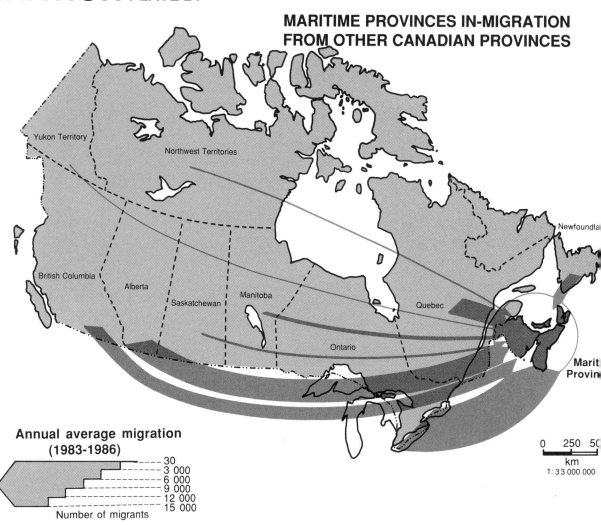

Annual average migration (1983-1986)

- 30
- 3 000
- 6 000
- 9 000
- 12 000
- 15 000

Number of migrants

0   250   50
km
1 : 33 000 000

MARITIME PROVINCES OUT-MIGRATION TO OTHER CANADIAN PROVINCES

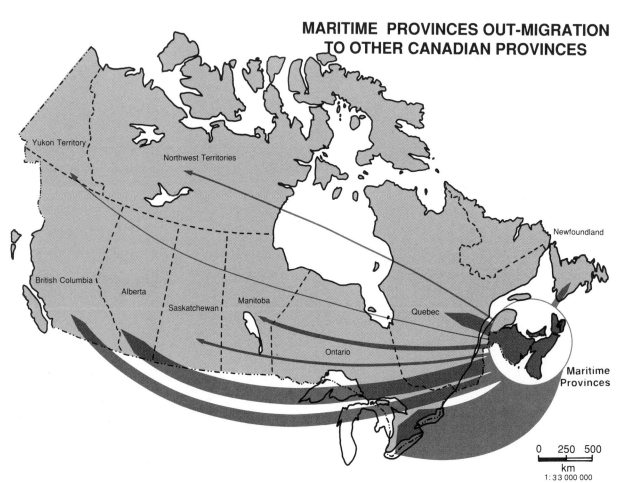

0   250   500
km
1 : 33 000 000

INTERPROVINCIAL NET MIGRATION SINCE 1961

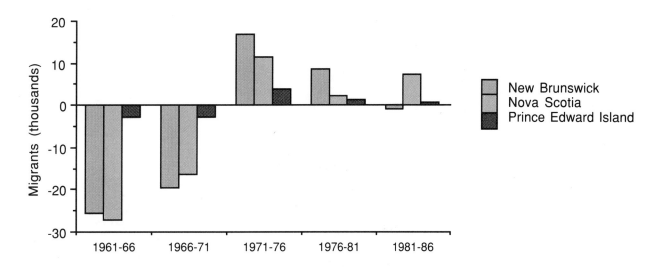

New Brunswick
Nova Scotia
Prince Edward Island

IMMIGRATION

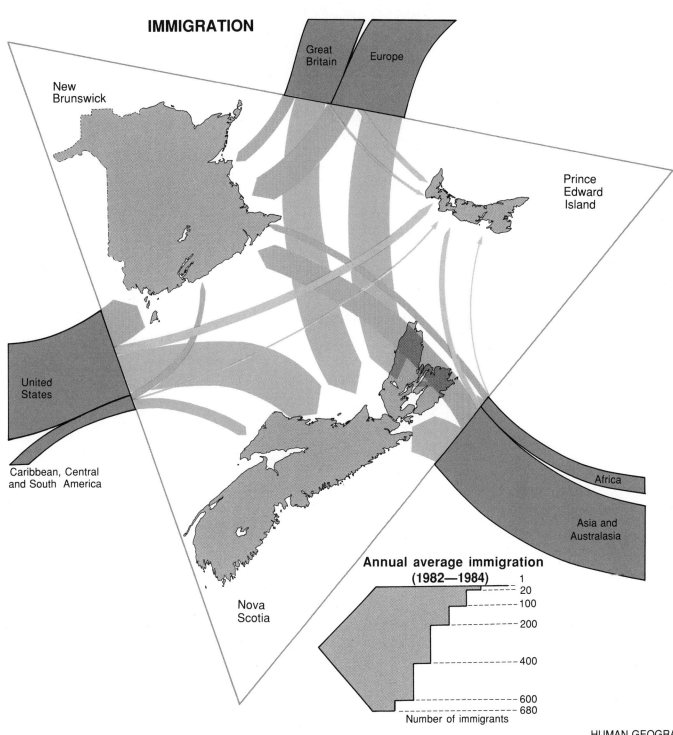

New Brunswick

Great Britain

Europe

Prince Edward Island

United States

Caribbean, Central and South America

Africa

Asia and Australasia

Nova Scotia

Annual average immigration (1982—1984)

1
20
100
200
400
600
680

Number of immigrants

MIGRATION WITHIN THE MARITIME PROVINCES PLATE 25

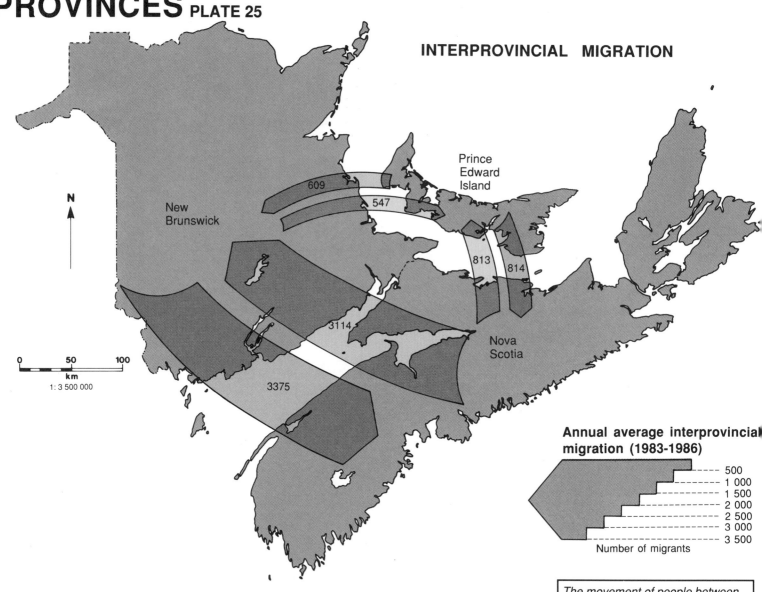

INTERPROVINCIAL MIGRATION

609
547
813
814
3114
3375

New Brunswick

Prince Edward Island

Nova Scotia

N

0   50   100
km
1: 3 500 000

Annual average interprovincial migration (1983-1986)

500
1 000
1 500
2 000
2 500
3 000
3 500

Number of migrants

The movement of people between the Maritime Provinces is featured above. Bar graphs show the age of migrants moving within each province (intra-provincial), between provinces (interprovincial) and from other countries (immigration). On the right, maps show intra-provincial migration (in and out) by counties.

AGE OF MIGRANTS OVER 15 YEARS, BY AGE GROUPS AND TYPE OF MIGRANT (1981)

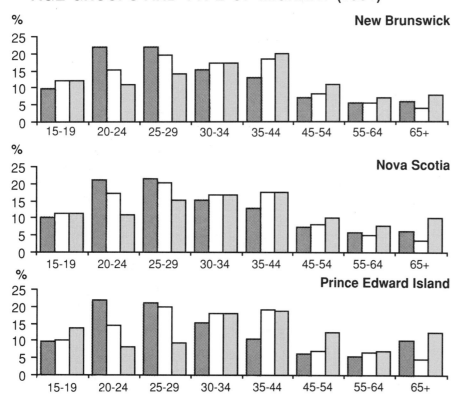

New Brunswick

Nova Scotia

Prince Edward Island

■ Intra-provincial
□ Interprovincial
▨ International

IN-MIGRATION BY COUNTY FOR EACH MARITIME PROVINCE (1981)

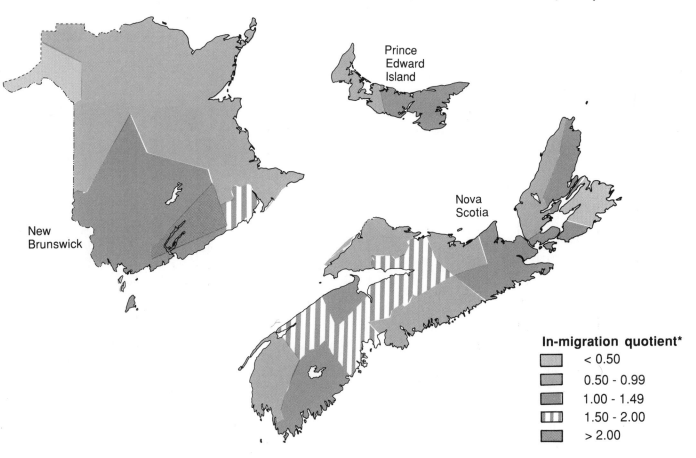

Prince
Edward
Island

Nova
Scotia

New
Brunswick

In-migration quotient*

- < 0.50
- 0.50 - 0.99
- 1.00 - 1.49
- 1.50 - 2.00
- > 2.00

* A quotient of 1.00 represents the provincial norm. Any quotients greater than 1 represent migration amounts, either in or out, greater than the norm; quotients less than 1 indicate migration amounts less than the norm for the province. For example, an in-migration quotient of 2 would indicate that twice as many people migrated to that county than the provincial norm. Similarly, an out-migration quotient of 0.5 would indicate that half as many people migrated from that county than the provincial norm.

OUT-MIGRATION BY COUNTY FOR EACH MARITIME PROVINCE (1981)

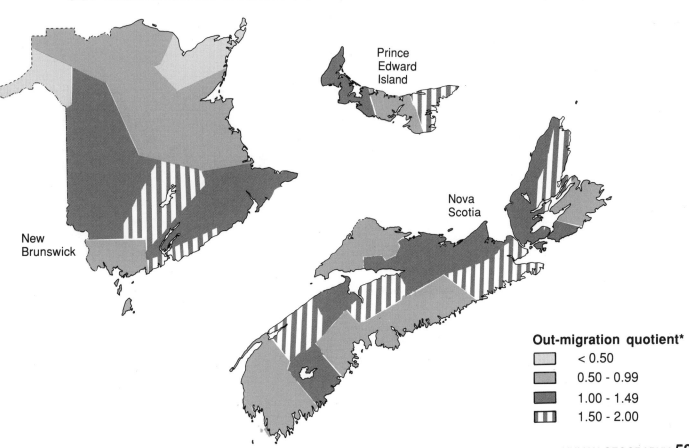

Prince
Edward
Island

Nova
Scotia

New
Brunswick

Out-migration quotient*

- < 0.50
- 0.50 - 0.99
- 1.00 - 1.49
- 1.50 - 2.00

AVERAGE NUMBER OF PERSONS PER FAMILY

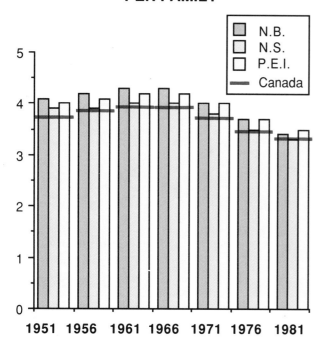

Legend:
- N.B.
- N.S.
- P.E.I.
- Canada

LIFE EXPECTANCY AT BIRTH

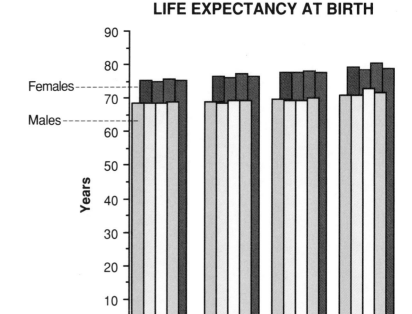

Females
Males

Years

1966   1971   1976   1981

This plate shows aspects of the quality of life in the Maritime Provinces. The main components are family size, life expectancy, suicides and social service expenditures. The crime page (right) with its map and graphs indicates a wide variety of crimes committed in Maritime communities.

SOCIAL SERVICE EXPENDITURES* AS A PER CENT OF GOVERNMENT GROSS GENERAL EXPENDITURES

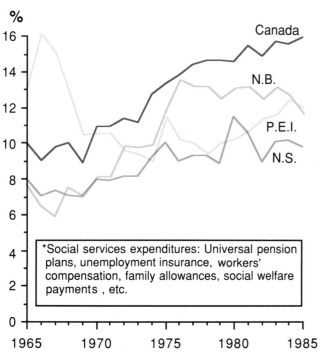

%

Canada
N.B.
P.E.I.
N.S.

*Social services expenditures: Universal pension plans, unemployment insurance, workers' compensation, family allowances, social welfare payments , etc.

SUICIDE RATE

Per 1000 population

Canada
Maritimes

1965   1970   1975   1980   198

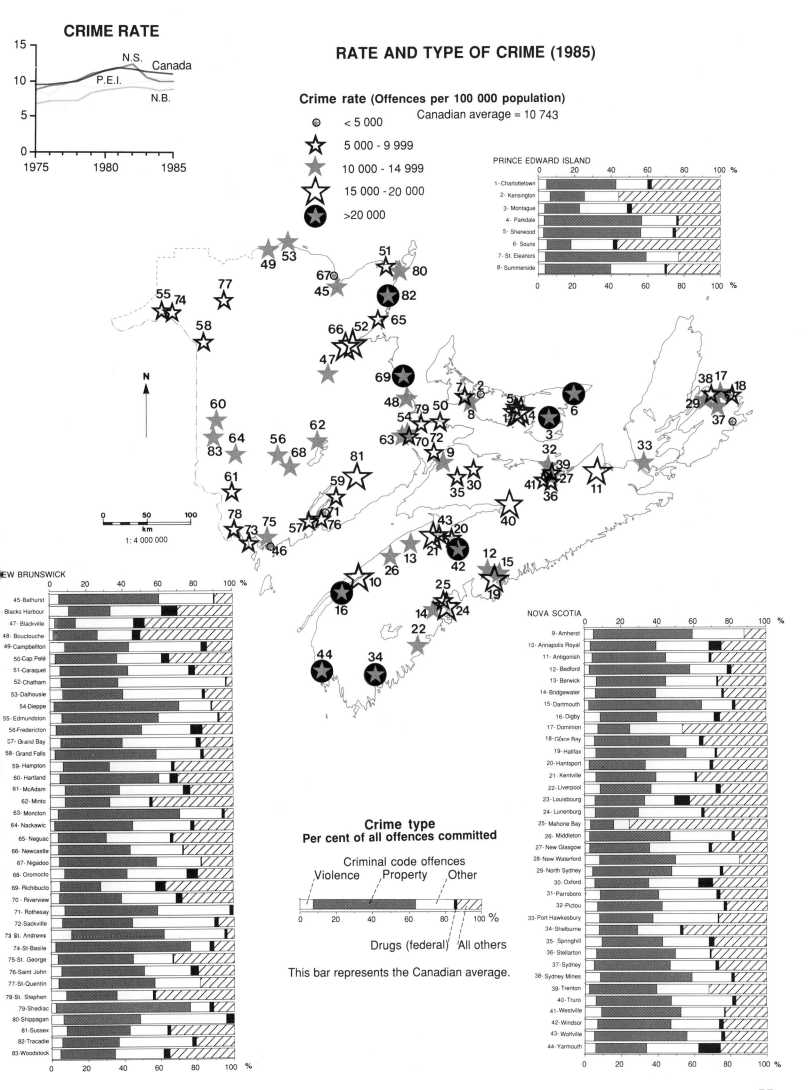

CRIME RATE

15

N.S.

Canada

10

P.E.I.

N.B.

5

0

1975   1980   1985

RATE AND TYPE OF CRIME (1985)

Crime rate (Offences per 100 000 population)
Canadian average = 10 743

- < 5 000
- 5 000 - 9 999
- 10 000 - 14 999
- 15 000 - 20 000
- >20 000

PRINCE EDWARD ISLAND

	0	20	40	60	80	100 %
1 - Charlottetown						
2 - Kensington						
3 - Montague						
4 - Parkdale						
5 - Sherwood						
6 - Souris						
7 - St. Eleanors						
8 - Summerside						

Crime type
Per cent of all offences committed

Criminal code offences

Violence   Property   Other

| 0 | 20 | 40 | 60 | 80 | 100 % |

Drugs (federal)   All others

This bar represents the Canadian average.

NEW BRUNSWICK

	0	20	40	60	80	100 %
45 - Bathurst						
46 - Blacks Harbour						
47 - Blackville						
48 - Bouctouche						
49 - Campbellton						
50 - Cap Pelé						
51 - Caraquet						
52 - Chatham						
53 - Dalhousie						
54 - Dieppe						
55 - Edmundston						
56 - Fredericton						
57 - Grand Bay						
58 - Grand Falls						
59 - Hampton						
60 - Hartland						
61 - McAdam						
62 - Minto						
63 - Moncton						
64 - Nackawic						
65 - Neguac						
66 - Newcastle						
67 - Nigadoo						
68 - Oromocto						
69 - Richibucto						
70 - Riverview						
71 - Rothesay						
72 - Sackville						
73 - St. Andrews						
74 - St-Basile						
75 - St. George						
76 - Saint John						
77 - St-Quentin						
78 - St. Stephen						
79 - Shediac						
80 - Shippagan						
81 - Sussex						
82 - Tracadie						
83 - Woodstock						

NOVA SCOTIA

	0	20	40	60	80	100 %
9 - Amherst						
10 - Annapolis Royal						
11 - Antigonish						
12 - Bedford						
13 - Berwick						
14 - Bridgewater						
15 - Dartmouth						
16 - Digby						
17 - Dominion						
18 - Glace Bay						
19 - Halifax						
20 - Hantsport						
21 - Kentville						
22 - Liverpool						
23 - Louisbourg						
24 - Lunenburg						
25 - Mahone Bay						
26 - Middleton						
27 - New Glasgow						
28 - New Waterford						
29 - North Sydney						
30 - Oxford						
31 - Parrsboro						
32 - Pictou						
33 - Port Hawkesbury						
34 - Shelburne						
35 - Springhill						
36 - Stellarton						
37 - Sydney						
38 - Sydney Mines						
39 - Trenton						
40 - Truro						
41 - Westville						
42 - Windsor						
43 - Wolfville						
44 - Yarmouth						

FEDERAL ELECTIONS PLATE 27

ELECTIONS BY RIDINGS

／ Riding boundary
R Riding boundary change since previous election
2 Dual riding (2 members returned)

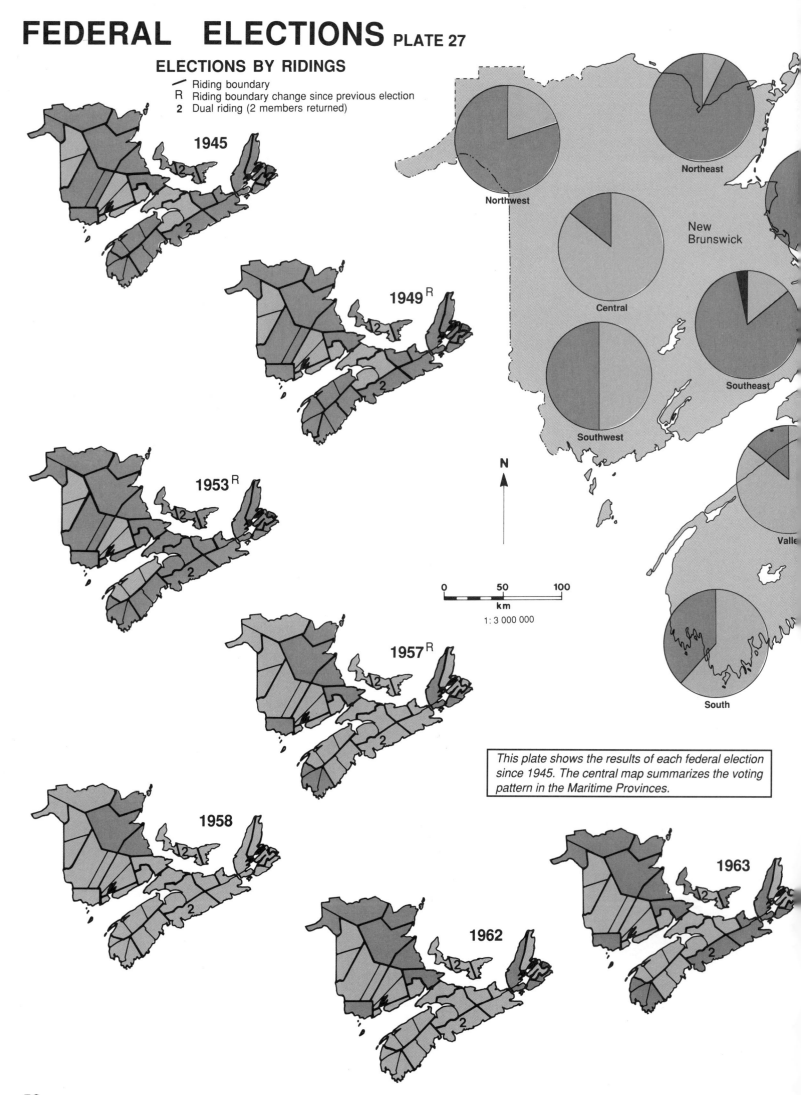

1945

1949 R

1953 R

1957 R

1958

Northwest

Northeast

New Brunswick

Central

Southeast

Southwest

South

Valle

N

0   50   100
km
1 : 3 000 000

This plate shows the results of each federal election
since 1945. The central map summarizes the voting
pattern in the Maritime Provinces.

1962

1963

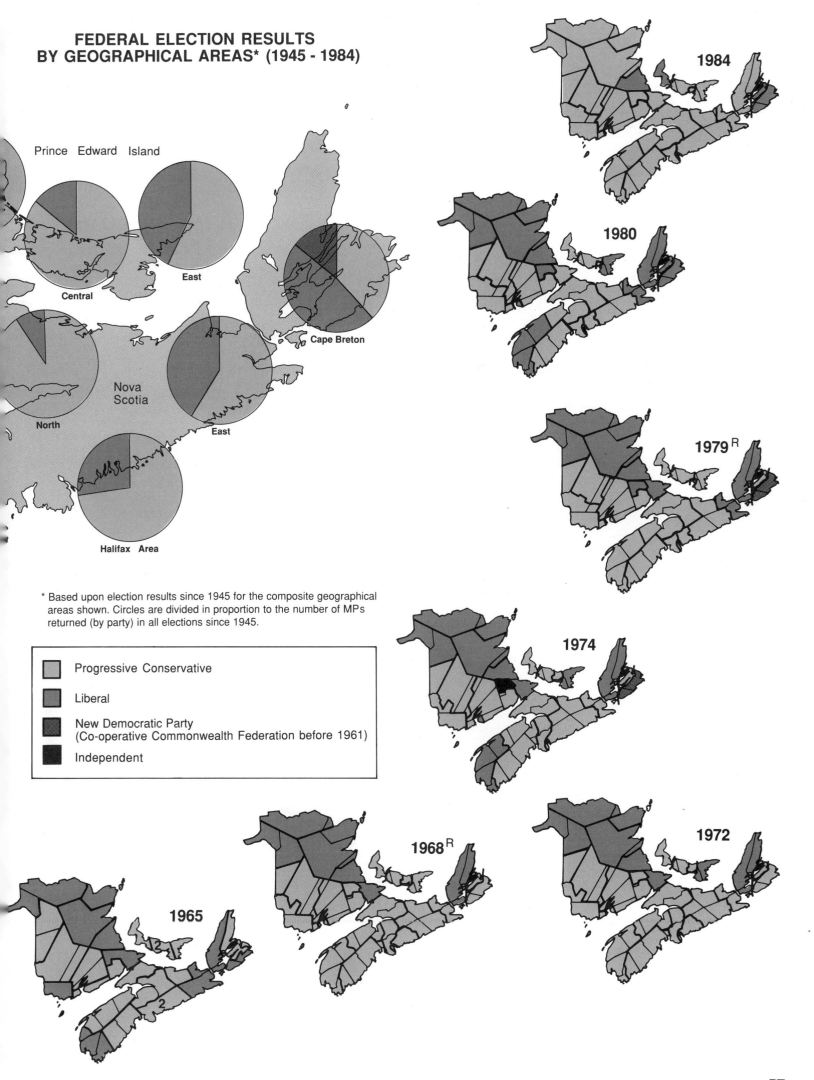

FEDERAL ELECTION RESULTS
BY GEOGRAPHICAL AREAS* (1945 - 1984)

Prince Edward Island

Central

East

Cape Breton

Nova Scotia

North

East

Halifax Area

1984

1980

1979 R

1974

1972

1968 R

1965

* Based upon election results since 1945 for the composite geographical areas shown. Circles are divided in proportion to the number of MPs returned (by party) in all elections since 1945.

Progressive Conservative

Liberal

New Democratic Party
(Co-operative Commonwealth Federation before 1961)

Independent

CULTURE AND IDENTITIES PLATE 28
EXAMPLES OF THE DIVERSITY OF FESTIVALS AND EVENTS (1987)

NEW BRUNSWICK

Date	Event	Location
Jan 30 - Feb 7	Ground Hog Festival	Beresford
Feb	Le Théatre Populaire d'Acadie	throughout N.B.
Feb 5 - 8	Warm Up Weekend	Saint John
Feb 14	Blueberry Maple Fest Talent Night and Cake and Ice Cream Sale	Elgin
Mar 28-29	Maple Sugar Bush Weekend	Kings Landing
Apr 28 - May 3	11th Annual YMCA Quilt Fair	Moncton
May 21 - 24	Cathedral Festival of the Arts	Fredericton
June 12 - 21	Marshlands Frolics	Sackville
June 26 - July 4	Railroad Days	Moncton
June 29 - July 5	Salmon Festival	Campbellton
July 1	Canada Day Celebrations	throughout N.B.
July 1 - 6	River Jubilee	Fredericton
July 3 - 4	14th Annual Antiques Show	St. Andrews
July 7 - 12	Lobster Festival	Shediac
July 12 - 19	Provincial Fisheries Festival	Shippagan
July 19 - 25	Loyalist Days Festival	Saint John
July 23 - 27	Peat Moss Festival	Lamèque
July 24 - Aug 1	Old Home Week	Woodstock
July 27 - Aug 2	Brussels Sprouts Festival	Rogersville
July 29 - Aug 2	Foire Brayonne	Edmundston
July - Aug	Parlee Beach Summer Theatre	Parlee Beach
Aug 3 - 7	Miramichi Folk Song Festival	Newcastle
Aug 7 - 16	Acadian Festival	Caraquet
Aug 9 - 22	Festival by the Sea	Saint John
Aug 23 - 29	Atlantic National Exhibition	Saint John
Sept 5	North American Sardine Packing Championship	Black's Harbour
Sept 10 - 12	Queens County Fair	Gagetown
Sept 17 - 19	Sussex Fall Fair and Atlantic Hot Air Balloon Festival	Sussex
Sept 26 - 27	Lumberman's Days	Kings Landing
Oct 24 - Nov 1	Maritime Winter Fair	Moncton

NOVA SCOTIA

Date	Event	Location
Jan 30 - Feb 8	Dartmouth Winter Carnival	Dartmouth
Feb 23 - Feb 28	Nova Scotia Kiwanis Music Festival	Halifax
March 24 - Apr 11	Maple Syrup Festivals of N.S.	Western and central N.S.
Apr 2 - Apr 4	Maritime Antique Dealers' Association Show and Sale	Halifax
May 9	Pig Out and Horse Pull	Caledonia
May 28 - June 1	Annapolis Valley Apple Blossom Festival	Windsor to Digby
June 12 - June 14	Nova Scotia Forestry Exhibition	Windsor
June 27 - July 2	Nova Scotia Tattoo	Halifax
June 27 - July 5	Mabou Ceilidh	Mabou
July 1	Canada Day celebrations	throughout N.S.
July 7 - July 12	Festival Acadien de Clare	Clare
July 9 - July 12	Antigonish Highland Games	Antigonish
July 10 - July 11	Maritime Old Time Fiddling Contest	Dartmouth
mid July - mid Aug	Centre Bras d'Or Festival of the Arts	Baddeck
July 18 - Aug 29	King's Festival '87	Annapolis Royal
July 24 - July 26	16th Annual Nova Scotia Blue-grass and Oldtime Music Festival	Ardoise
Aug 1 - Aug 8	Annual (14th) Action Week	Sydney
Aug 3 - Aug 8	Western Nova Scotia Exhibition	Yarmouth
Aug 20 - Aug 23	Cumberland County Blueberry Harvest Festival	throughout central N.S.
Aug 23	Clam Harbour Beach Sand Sculpturing Contest	Clam Harbour
Sept 5	Annual (50th) Western Kings Community Fair	Tremont
Sept 23 - Sept 27	Nova Scotia Fisheries Exhibition and Fishermen's Reunion	Lunenburg
Sept 19 - Sept 20	Shearwater International Air Show 1987	Shearwater
Oct 10 - Oct 17	Atlantic Winter Fair	Halifax
Oct 24	Pomorze Polish Harvest Dance	Halifax
Nov 5 - Nov 8	Christmas at the Forum: The Festival of Crafts, Antiques, Art and Foods	Halifax

PRINCE EDWARD ISLAND

Date	Event	Location
May 21 - 31	Creative Youth Fair	Summers
June 19 - 21	St. Lawrence Scallop Festival	St. Lawre
June 25 - Oct 10	The Charlottetown Festival	Charlotte
June 26 - 28	Tignish Irish Moss Festival	Tignish
June 29 - July 1	Bedeque Days	Bedeque
July 1	Canada Day Celebrations	througho
July 1 - 6	Gateway Port Days	Borden
July 6 - 12	Somerset Festival	Kinkora
July 9 - 11	Belfast Lion's Day Pace	Belfast
July 11 - 12	P.E.I. Irish Folk Festival	Woodsto
July 15 - 19	Morell and Area North Side Strawberry Festival	Morell
July 19 - 25	Summerside Lobster Carnival and Livestock Exhibition	Summers
July 22 - 25	P.E.I. Potato Blossom Festival	O'Leary
July 30 - Aug 2	Northumberland Provincial Fisheries Exhibition	Murray P
Aug 1	Scottish Gathering and Highland Games	Eldon
Aug 5 - 9	Tyne Valley Oyster Festival	Tyne Val
Aug 7 - 9	St. Peter's Blueberry Festival	St. Peter
Aug 7 - 15	Old Home Week	Charlotte
Aug 9 -12	La Fête Acadienne	Tignish
Aug 15	28th Gold Cup and Saucer Harness Race	Charlotte
Aug 20 - 22	P.E.I. Plowing Match and Agricultural Fair	Dundas
Aug 20 - 26	Community Harvest Festival	Kensingt
Aug 26 - 27	Eastern Kings Exhibition	Souris
Sept 4 - 6	Le Festival Acadien de la Région Évangéline	Abram-V
Oct 24	Run for Pumpkins	Charlotte

IDENTITIES (1987)

Defined as the most common name in each community listed in telephone directory. This map gives no indication of actual numb of people, rather it shows the occurrence of surnames.

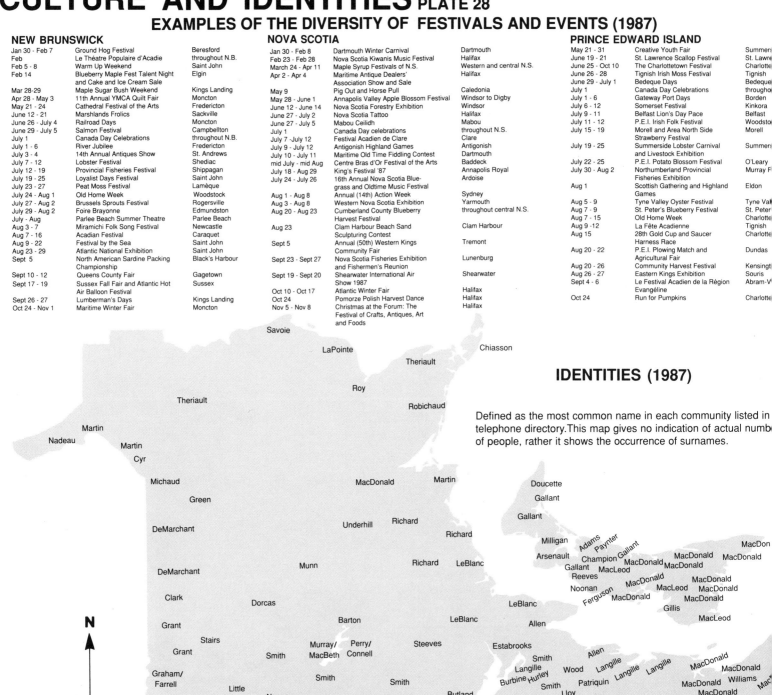

The IDENTITIES map (above) shows the most common name in each Maritime community. Other maps show the distribution of craft outlets, writers and theatres. A table to indicate the variety of cultural events is listed for each province.

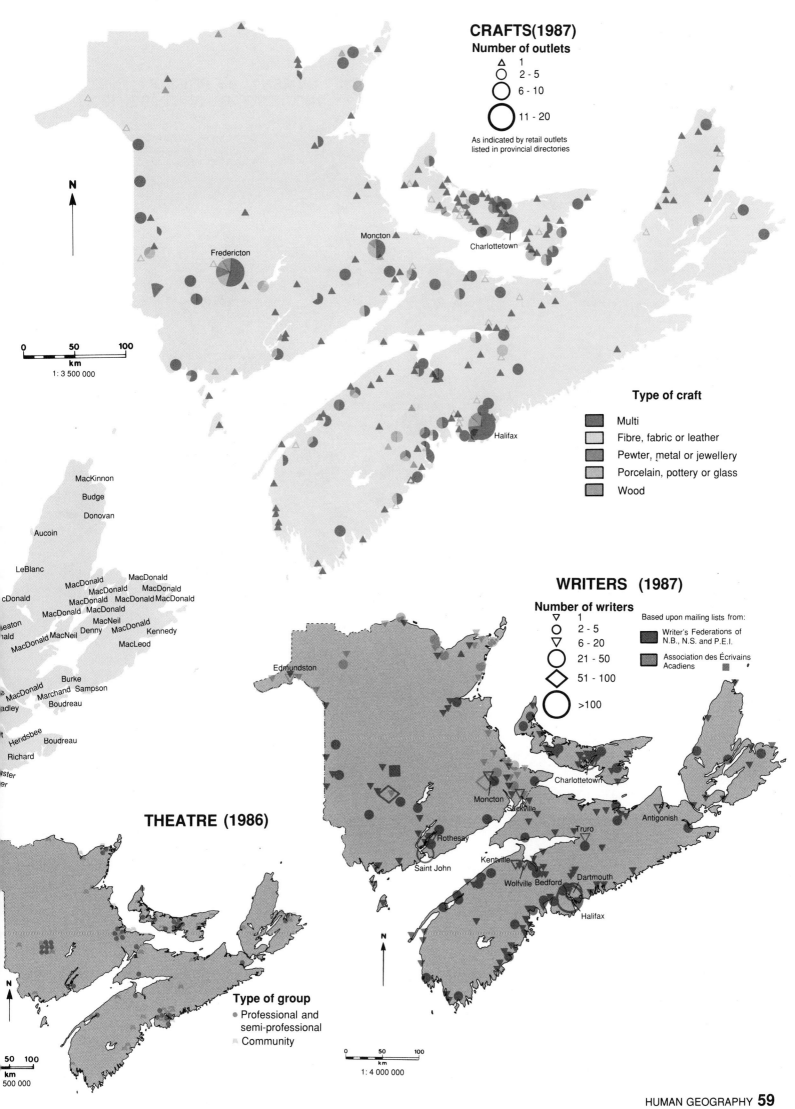

CRAFTS(1987)

Number of outlets

△ 1
○ 2 - 5
◯ 6 - 10
◯ 11 - 20

As indicated by retail outlets listed in provincial directories

Type of craft

■ Multi
□ Fibre, fabric or leather
■ Pewter, metal or jewellery
□ Porcelain, pottery or glass
■ Wood

Fredericton

Moncton

Charlottetown

Halifax

N

0 50 100
km
1: 3 500 000

MacKinnon
Budge
Donovan
Aucoin
LeBlanc
cDonald
MacDonald MacDonald
MacDonald MacDonald MacDonald
MacDonald MacDonald MacDonald
MacDonald MacDonald
MacNeil MacDonald
seaton
ald MacDonald MacNeil Denny MacDonald Kennedy
MacLeod
Burke
MacDonald Marchand Sampson
adley Boudreau
Hendsbee Boudreau
Richard
ster
er

WRITERS (1987)

Number of writers

▽ 1
○ 2 - 5
▽ 6 - 20
◯ 21 - 50
◇ 51 - 100
◯ >100

Based upon mailing lists from:

■ Writer's Federations of N.B., N.S. and P.E.I.
■ Association des Écrivains Acadiens

Edmundston
Charlottetown
Moncton
Sackville
Antigonish
Truro
Rothesay
Kentville
Saint John
Wolfville Bedford Dartmouth
Halifax

N

0 50 100
km
1: 4 000 000

THEATRE (1986)

Type of group

● Professional and semi-professional
▲ Community

N

50 100
km
500 000

EMPLOYMENT* BY PRIMARY, SECONDARY AND TERTIARY SECTORS (1981)

* For persons 15 years and older who are employed, except inmates of institutions.

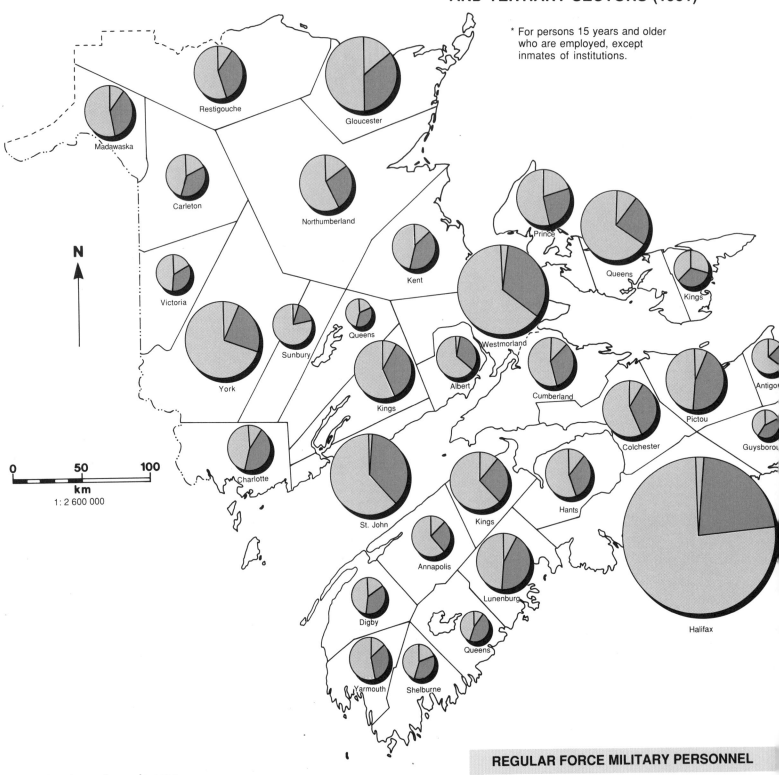

N

0 50 100
km
1: 2 600 000

Madawaska
Restigouche
Gloucester
Carleton
Northumberland
Victoria
Kent
Prince
Queens
Kings
Westmorland
Sunbury
Queens
York
Albert
Cumberland
Antigo
Kings
Pictou
Colchester
Charlotte
Guysborou
St. John
Hants
Annapolis
Kings
Halifax
Digby
Lunenburg
Queens
Yarmouth
Shelburne

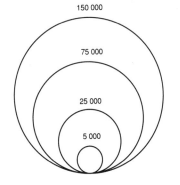

Number of employees

150 000
75 000
25 000
5 000

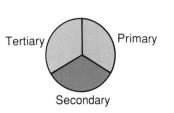

Employment type

Tertiary
Primary
Secondary

REGULAR FORCE MILITARY PERSONNEL

	N.B.	N.S.	P.E.I.
1981	4300	12925	875
1987	4500	12875	950
Locations	C.F.B. Chatham C.F.B. Gagetown C.F.B. Moncton	C.F.B Cornwallis C.F.B. Greenwood C.F.B. Halifax C.F.B. Shearwater C.F.S. Barrington C.F.S. Mill Cove C.F.S. Shelburne C.F.S. Sydney	C.F.B. Summers

C.F.B. Canadian Forces Base
C.F.S. Canadian Forces Station

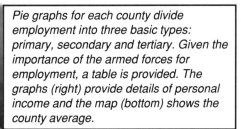

Pie graphs for each county divide employment into three basic types: primary, secondary and tertiary. Given the importance of the armed forces for employment, a table is provided. The graphs (right) provide details of personal income and the map (bottom) shows the county average.

PERSONAL INCOME BY GENDER*(1981)

Females
Males

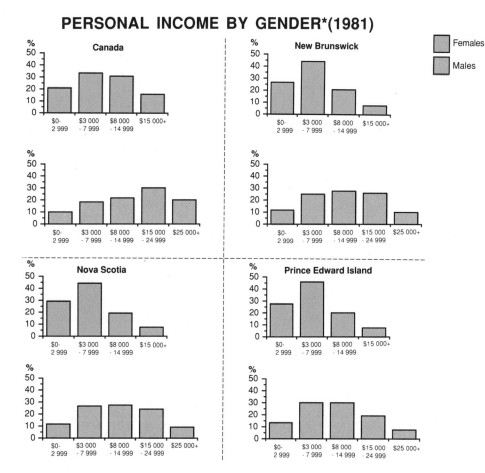

Canada

New Brunswick

Nova Scotia

Prince Edward Island

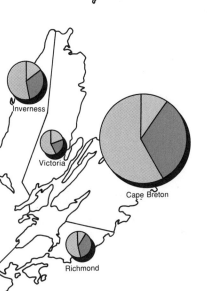

Inverness

Victoria

Cape Breton

Richmond

AVERAGE PERSONAL INCOME FROM THE LABOUR FORCE SURVEY

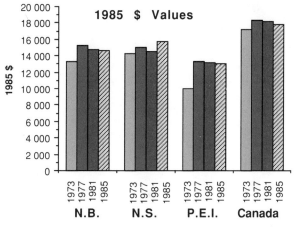

1985 $ Values

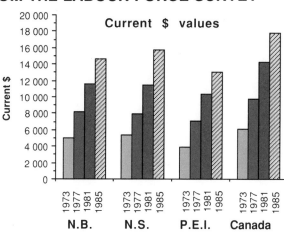

Current $ values

AVERAGE ANNUAL PERSONAL INCOME* (1981)

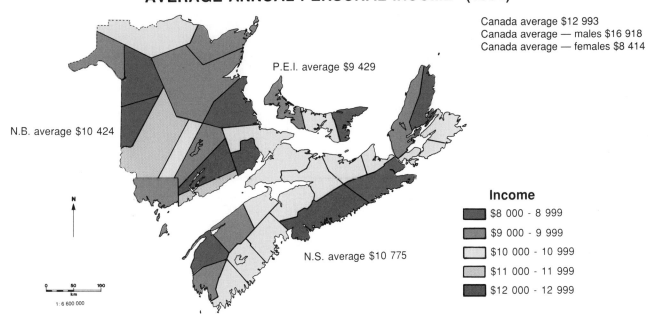

Canada average $12 993
Canada average — males $16 918
Canada average — females $8 414

P.E.I. average $9 429

N.B. average $10 424

N.S. average $10 775

Income
- $8 000 - 8 999
- $9 000 - 9 999
- $10 000 - 10 999
- $11 000 - 11 999
- $12 000 - 12 999

1: 6 600 000

UNEMPLOYMENT PLATE 30

ECONOMIC REGIONS OF THE MARITIME PROVINCES AND NATIONAL UNEMPLOYMENT* (1986)

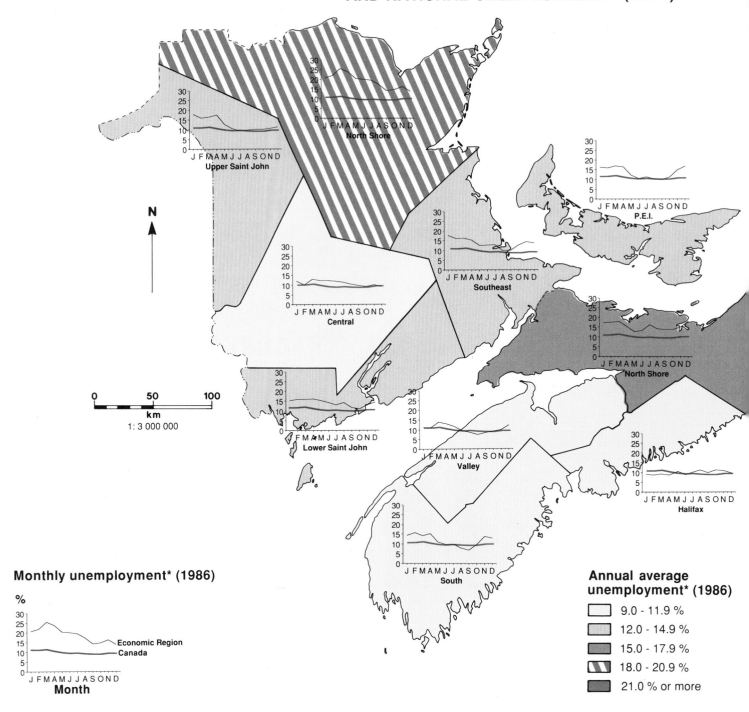

N

0   50   100
km
1 : 3 000 000

Upper Saint John

North Shore

Central

Southeast

P.E.I.

North Shore

Lower Saint John

Valley

South

Halifax

Monthly unemployment* (1986)

%

Economic Region

Canada

J F M A M J J A S O N D
Month

Annual average unemployment* (1986)

☐	9.0 - 11.9 %
☐	12.0 - 14.9 %
☐	15.0 - 17.9 %
☐	18.0 - 20.9 %
☐	21.0 % or more

MARITIME PROVINCES AND NATIONAL UNEMPLOYMENT* (1966-1986)

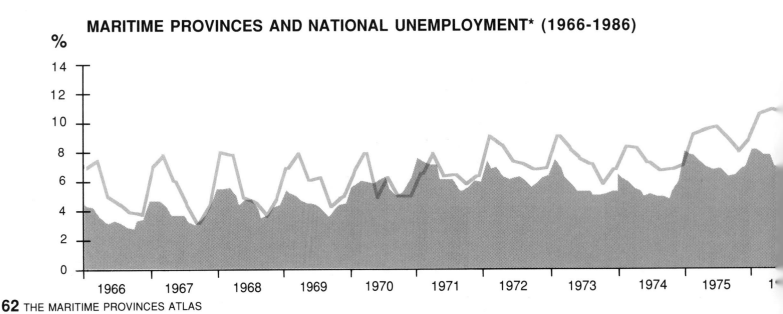

%

14

12

10

8

6

4

2

0

1966   1967   1968   1969   1970   1971   1972   1973   1974   1975

REGIONAL AND NATIONAL ANNUAL UNEMPLOYMENT*
(1966-1986)

* All unemployment figures are actual figures and not adjusted for seasonal changes.

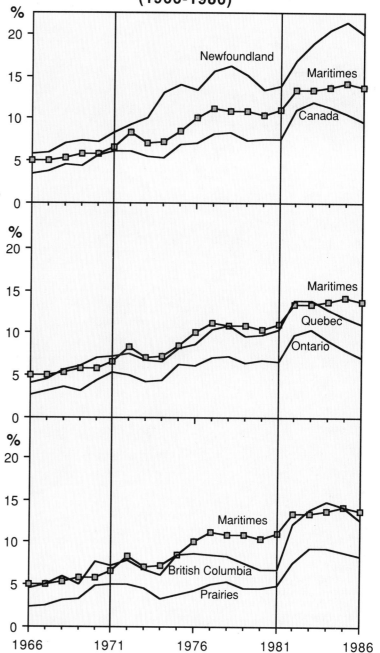

The map shows annual and monthly unemployment throughout the Maritimes. The long graph shows the long-term comparison between Maritimers who are out of work and the national average. The graphs (above) indicate that usually the unemployment rate in the Maritimes is the highest in the country, with the exception of Newfoundland.

UNEMPLOYMENT PAYMENTS
(In 1985 $ values)

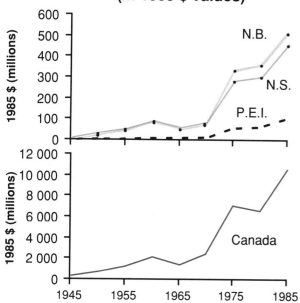

Maritimes

Canada

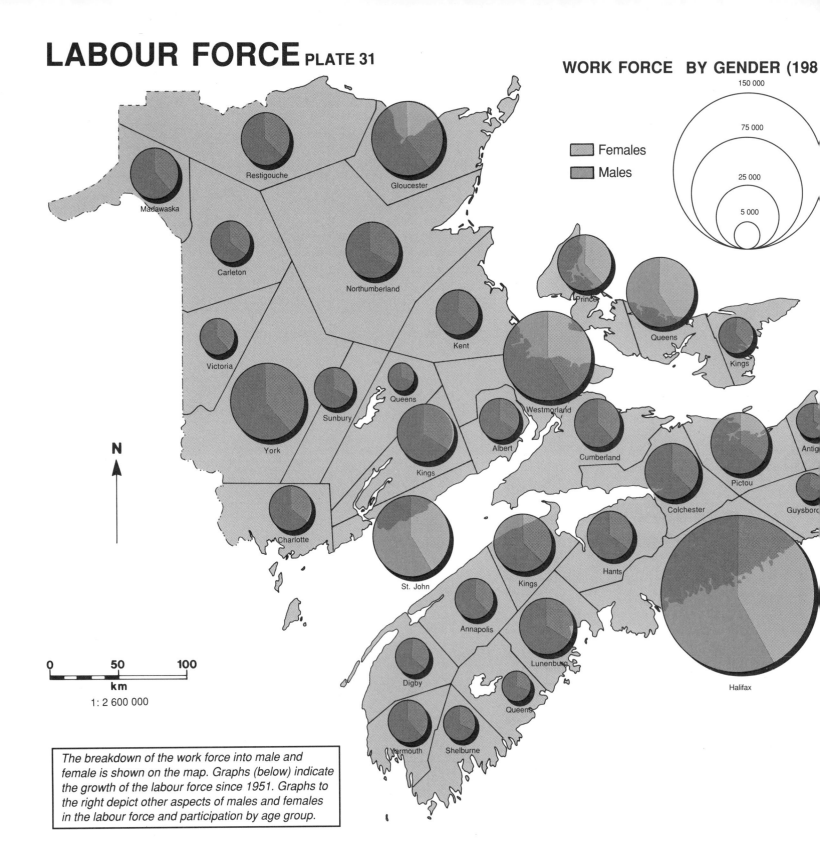

WORK FORCE BY GENDER (198

150 000

75 000

25 000

5 000

Females

Males

Madawaska
Restigouche
Gloucester
Carleton
Northumberland
Victoria
Kent
Queens
Sunbury
York
Albert
Kings
Charlotte
Westmorland
St. John
Cumberland
Prince
Queens
Kings
Antig
Pictou
Colchester
Guysbor
Hants
Kings
Annapolis
Lunenburg
Halifax
Digby
Queens
Yarmouth
Shelburne

N

0   50   100
km
1: 2 600 000

The breakdown of the work force into male and
female is shown on the map. Graphs (below) indicate
the growth of the labour force since 1951. Graphs to
the right depict other aspects of males and females
in the labour force and participation by age group.

GROWTH OF THE LABOUR FORCE

Labour force includes people 15 years and older who are
either employed or unemployed, except inmates of institutions.
For 1986 only, it excludes military personnel in the Armed Forces.

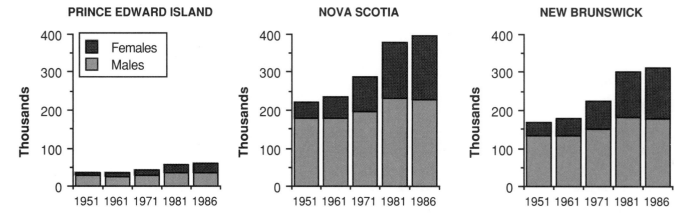

PRINCE EDWARD ISLAND

Females
Males

Thousands
400
300
200
100
0
1951 1961 1971 1981 1986

NOVA SCOTIA

Thousands
400
300
200
100
0
1951 1961 1971 1981 1986

NEW BRUNSWICK

Thousands
400
300
200
100
0
1951 1961 1971 1981 1986

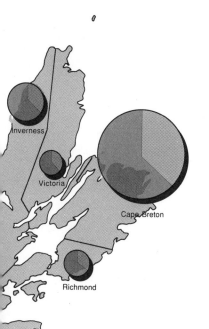

ork force includes people 15 years
nd older, except inmates of institutions,
ho are employed.

Inverness

Victoria

Cape Breton

Richmond

WORKING MALES AND FEMALES AS A PERCENTAGE OF THE POPULATION (15 years and older)

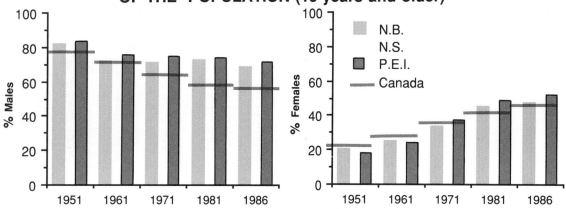

N.B.
N.S.
P.E.I.
Canada

MALES AND FEMALES AS A PERCENTAGE OF THE LABOUR FORCE

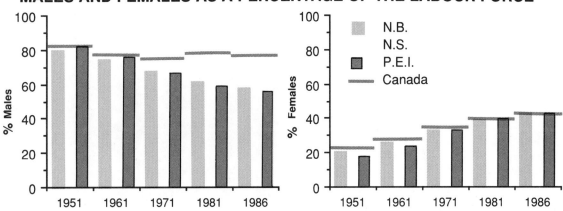

N.B.
N.S.
P.E.I.
Canada

PARTICIPATION BY AGE (1981)

Per cent of age group
participating in the labour force

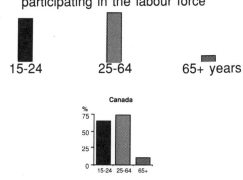

15-24   25-64   65+ years

Canada

NEW BRUNSWICK

Albert | Carleton | Charlotte
Gloucester | Kent | Kings
Madawaska | Northumberland | Queens
Restigouche | St. John | Sunbury
Victoria | Westmorland | York

PRINCE EDWARD ISLAND

Kings | Prince | Queens

NOVA SCOTIA

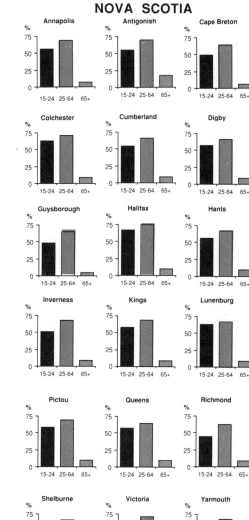

Annapolis | Antigonish | Cape Breton
Colchester | Cumberland | Digby
Guysborough | Halifax | Hants
Inverness | Kings | Lunenburg
Pictou | Queens | Richmond
Shelburne | Victoria | Yarmouth

MANUFACTURING ESTABLISHMENTS AND EMPLOYMENT PLATE 32

The importance of manufacturing in each county is shown on the map (below) and in the surrounding pie graphs. Other aspects of manufacturing are illustrated on the far right.

PREDOMINANT MANUFACTURING ACTIVITY

Counties are coloured according to predominant manufacturing activity defined as a composite of the value of goods shipped, value added and the number of employees.

Manufacturing activity

- Food, beverage and tobacco
- Leather, textiles and clothing
- Wood, furniture, paper, printing and publishing
- Primary and fabricated material
- Machinery, transport, electronic and electrical
- Rubber, petroleum and petrochemicals
- Non-metallic mineral and other manufacturing

Halifax, N.S.

Westmorland, N.B.

N

0   50   100
km
1: 3 000 000

Number of establishments in each size category (1983)

- 0-9 employees
- 10-49 employees
- 50-99 employees
- 100-499 employees
- 500 or more employees

Sunbury, N.B.
Albert, N.B.
Richmond, N.S.
Victoria, N.S.
Antigonish, N.S.
Queens, N.S.
Guysborough, N.S.
Inverness, N.S.
Queens, N.B.
Annapolis, N.S.
Kings, P.E.I.
Victoria, N.B.
Carleton, N.B.

Kent, N.B.
Charlotte, N.B.
Restigouche, N.B.
Hants, N.S.
Northumberland, N.B.
Kings, N.B.
Digby, N.S.
Madawaska, N.B.
Kings, N.

Restigouche
Madawaska
Gloucester
Victoria
Northumberland
Carleton
York
Kent
Queens
Sunbury
Albert
Kings
Charlotte
St. John
Prince
Queens
Westmorland
Kings
Annapolis
Cumberland
Colchester
Hants
Pictou
Antigo
Kings
Digby
Lunenburg
Halifax
Yarmouth
Queens
Shelburne

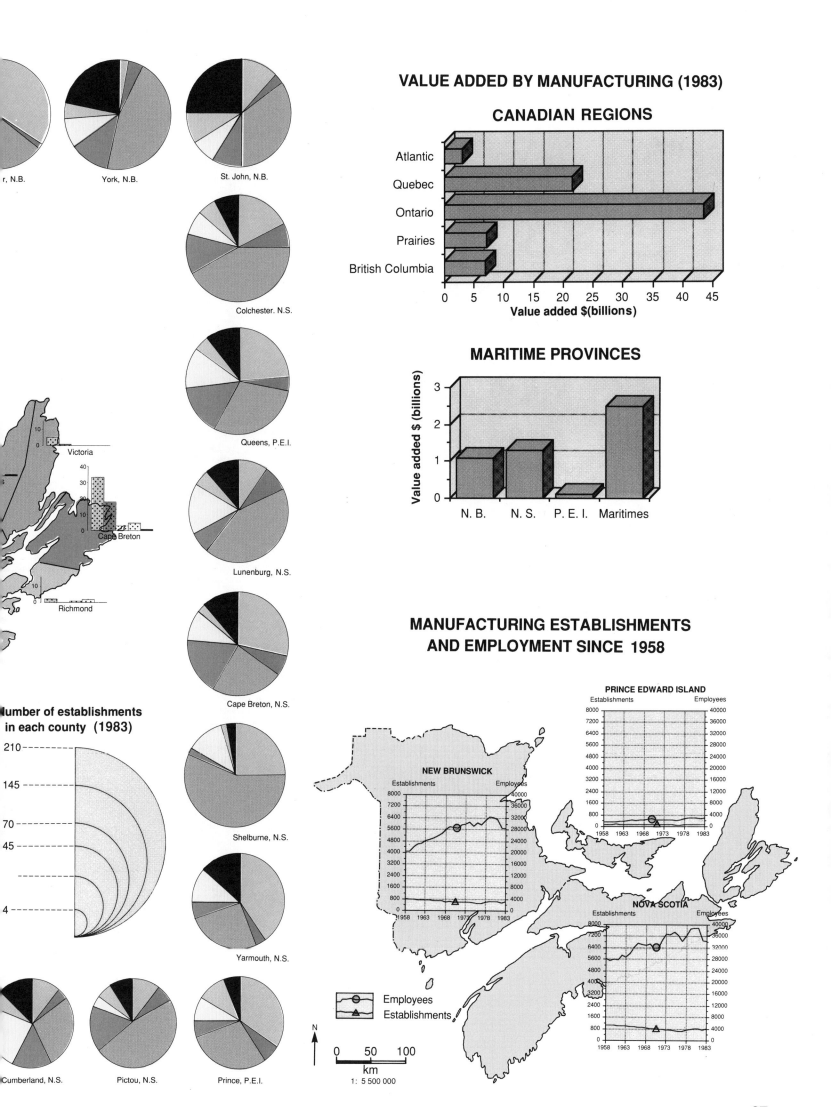

r, N.B.

York, N.B.

St. John, N.B.

Colchester. N.S.

Queens, P.E.I.

Lunenburg, N.S.

Cape Breton, N.S.

Shelburne, N.S.

Yarmouth, N.S.

Cumberland, N.S.

Pictou, N.S.

Prince, P.E.I.

Victoria

Cape Breton

Richmond

Number of establishments in each county (1983)

210
145
70
45
4

VALUE ADDED BY MANUFACTURING (1983)

CANADIAN REGIONS

Atlantic
Quebec
Ontario
Prairies
British Columbia

0   5   10   15   20   25   30   35   40   45
Value added $(billions)

MARITIME PROVINCES

Value added $ (billions)

3

2

1

0

N. B.   N. S.   P. E. I.   Maritimes

MANUFACTURING ESTABLISHMENTS AND EMPLOYMENT SINCE 1958

PRINCE EDWARD ISLAND
Establishments   Employees
8000   40000
7200   36000
6400   32000
5600   28000
4800   24000
4000   20000
3200   16000
2400   12000
1600   8000
800   4000
0   0
1958 1963 1968 1973 1978 1983

NEW BRUNSWICK
Establishments   Employees
8000   40000
7200   36000
6400   32000
5600   28000
4800   24000
4000   20000
3200   16000
2400   12000
1600   8000
800   4000
0   0
1958 1963 1968 1973 1978 1983

NOVA SCOTIA
Establishments   Employees
8000   40000
7200   36000
6400   32000
5600   28000
4800   24000
4000   20000
3200   16000
2400   12000
1600   8000
800   4000
0   0
1958 1963 1968 1973 1978 1983

○ Employees
△ Establishments

N

0   50   100
km
1: 5 500 000

RETAIL TRADE PLATE 33

The main map shows major retail trade centres with the approximate area they serve. The map in the upper right shows the floor space for rent in Maritime shopping malls. The two insets are examples of just how far people are likely to travel to buy bread or large appliances.

RETAIL SALES CENTRES WITH ESTIMATED TRADE AREAS

Research: H. A. Millward, 1987

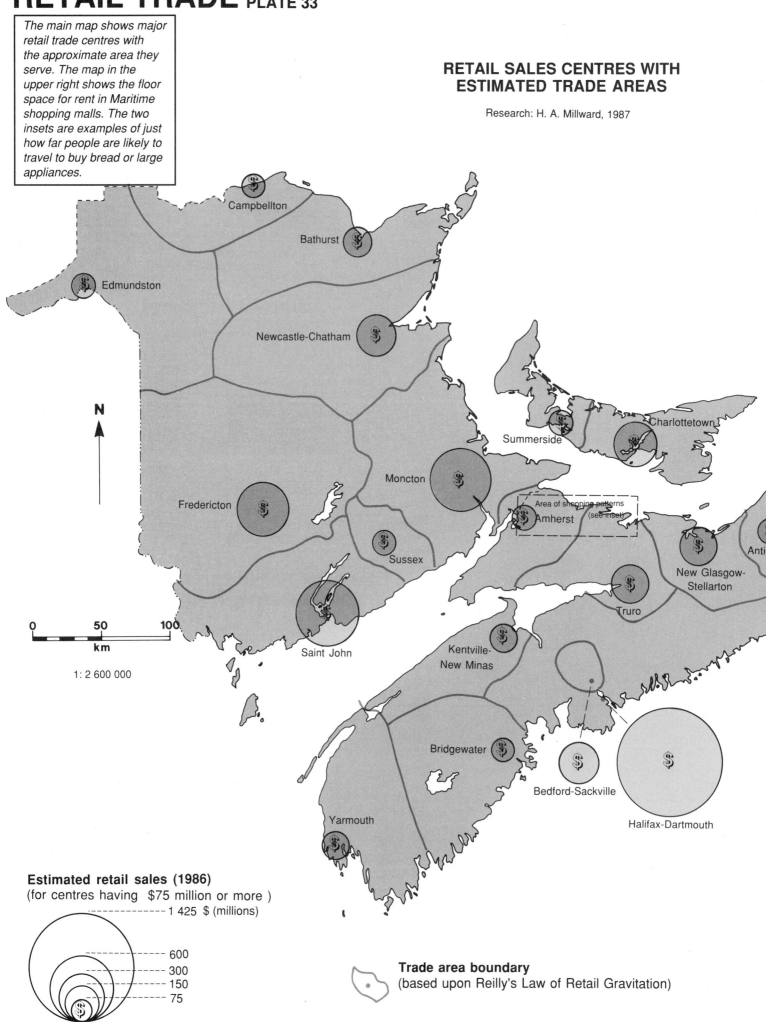

N

Campbellton

Bathurst

Edmundston

Newcastle-Chatham

Summerside

Charlottetown

Moncton

Fredericton

Amherst

Area of shopping patterns (see inset)

New Glasgow-Stellarton

Antigor

Sussex

Truro

Saint John

Kentville-New Minas

Bridgewater

Bedford-Sackville

Halifax-Dartmouth

Yarmouth

0   50   100
km

1: 2 600 000

Estimated retail sales (1986)
(for centres having $75 million or more)

- - - - - - - - - - 1 425 $ (millions)

- - - - - 600
- - - - - 300
- - - - - 150
- - - - - 75

Trade area boundary
(based upon Reilly's Law of Retail Gravitation)

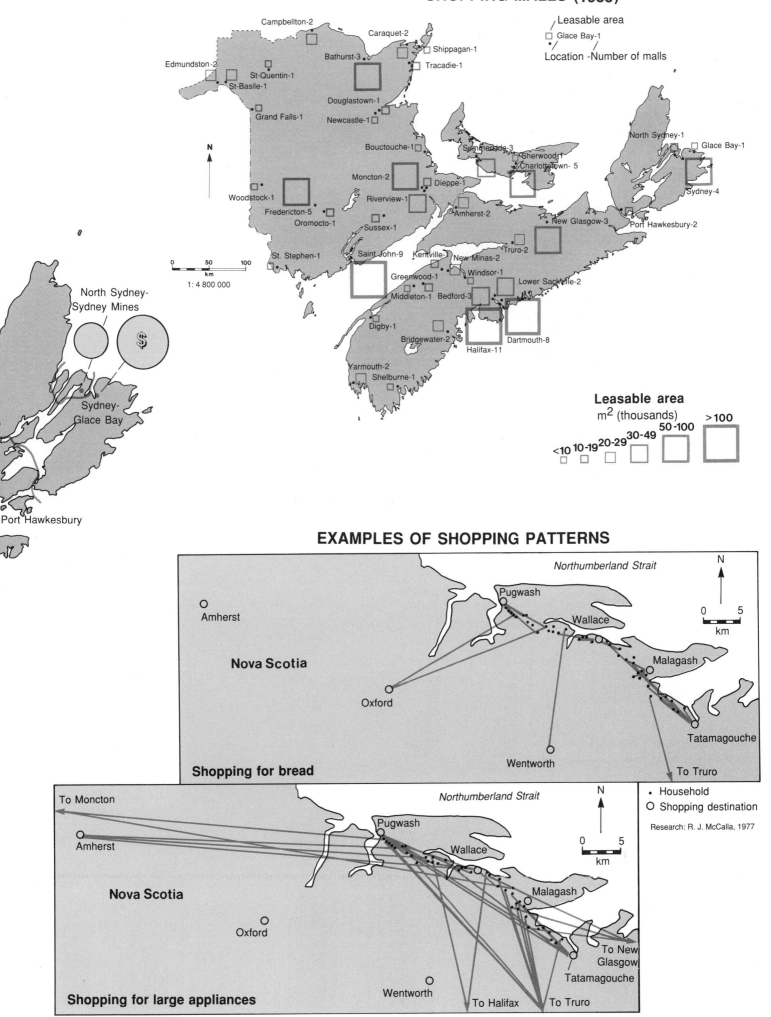

SHOPPING MALLS (1985)

Leasable area
☐ Glace Bay-1

Location -Number of malls

Campbellton-2
Caraquet-2
Bathurst-3
Shippagan-1
Edmundston-2
St-Quentin-1
Tracadie-1
St-Basile-1
Douglastown-1
Grand Falls-1
Newcastle-1
Bouctouche-1
Summerside-3
North Sydney-1
Glace Bay-1
Sherwood-1
Charlottetown- 5
Moncton-2
Dieppe-1
Sydney-4
Woodstock-1
Riverview-1
Port Hawkesbury-2
Fredericton-5
Amherst-2
New Glasgow-3
Oromocto-1
Sussex-1
Truro-2
St. Stephen-1
Saint John-9
Kentville-1
New Minas-2
Windsor-1
Greenwood-1
Lower Sackville-2
Middleton-1
Bedford-3
Digby-1
Dartmouth-8
Bridgewater-2
Halifax-11
Yarmouth-2
Shelburne-1

N

0   50   100
km
1: 4 800 000

North Sydney-
Sydney Mines

$

Sydney-
Glace Bay

Port Hawkesbury

Leasable area
m² (thousands)

>100

50 -100

30-49

<10 10-19 20-29

EXAMPLES OF SHOPPING PATTERNS

Northumberland Strait

N

0   5
km

Amherst

Nova Scotia

Pugwash

Wallace

Malagash

Oxford

Wentworth

Tatamagouche

To Truro

Shopping for bread

• Household
O Shopping destination

Research: R. J. McCalla, 1977

To Moncton

Northumberland Strait

N

0   5
km

Amherst

Pugwash

Wallace

Nova Scotia

Oxford

Malagash

Wentworth

To New
Glasgow

Tatamagouche

To Halifax   To Truro

Shopping for large appliances

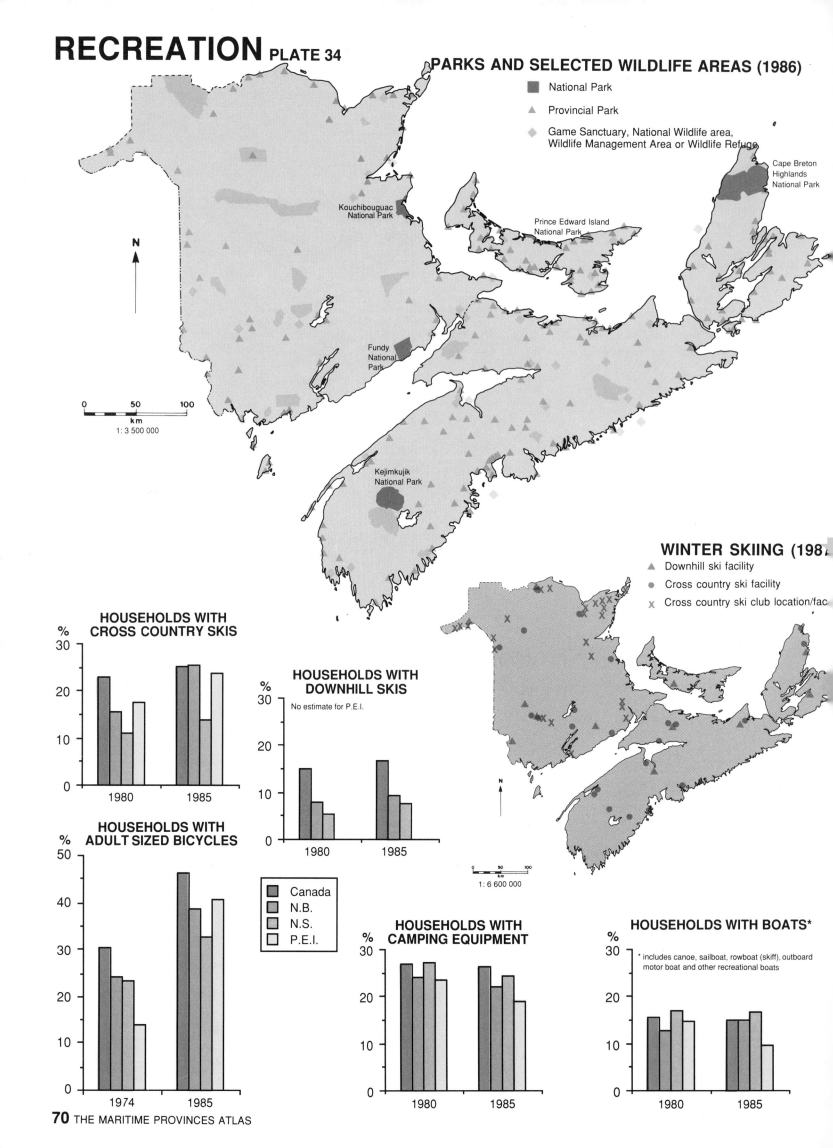

PARKS AND SELECTED WILDLIFE AREAS (1986)

- National Park
- ▲ Provincial Park
- ◆ Game Sanctuary, National Wildlife area, Wildlife Management Area or Wildlife Refuge

Kouchibouguac National Park

Cape Breton Highlands National Park

Prince Edward Island National Park

Fundy National Park

Kejimkujik National Park

0   50   100
km
1: 3 500 000

WINTER SKIING (1982)

- ▲ Downhill ski facility
- ● Cross country ski facility
- ✕ Cross country ski club location/fac...

N

0   50   100
km
1: 6 600 000

HOUSEHOLDS WITH CROSS COUNTRY SKIS

%
30
20
10
0
    1980   1985

HOUSEHOLDS WITH DOWNHILL SKIS

%
30
No estimate for P.E.I.
20
10
0
    1980   1985

HOUSEHOLDS WITH ADULT SIZED BICYCLES

%
50
40
30
20
10
0
    1974   1985

Legend:
- Canada
- N.B.
- N.S.
- P.E.I.

HOUSEHOLDS WITH CAMPING EQUIPMENT

%
30
20
10
0
    1980   1985

HOUSEHOLDS WITH BOATS*

%
30
* includes canoe, sailboat, rowboat (skiff), outboard motor boat and other recreational boats
20
10
0
    1980   1985

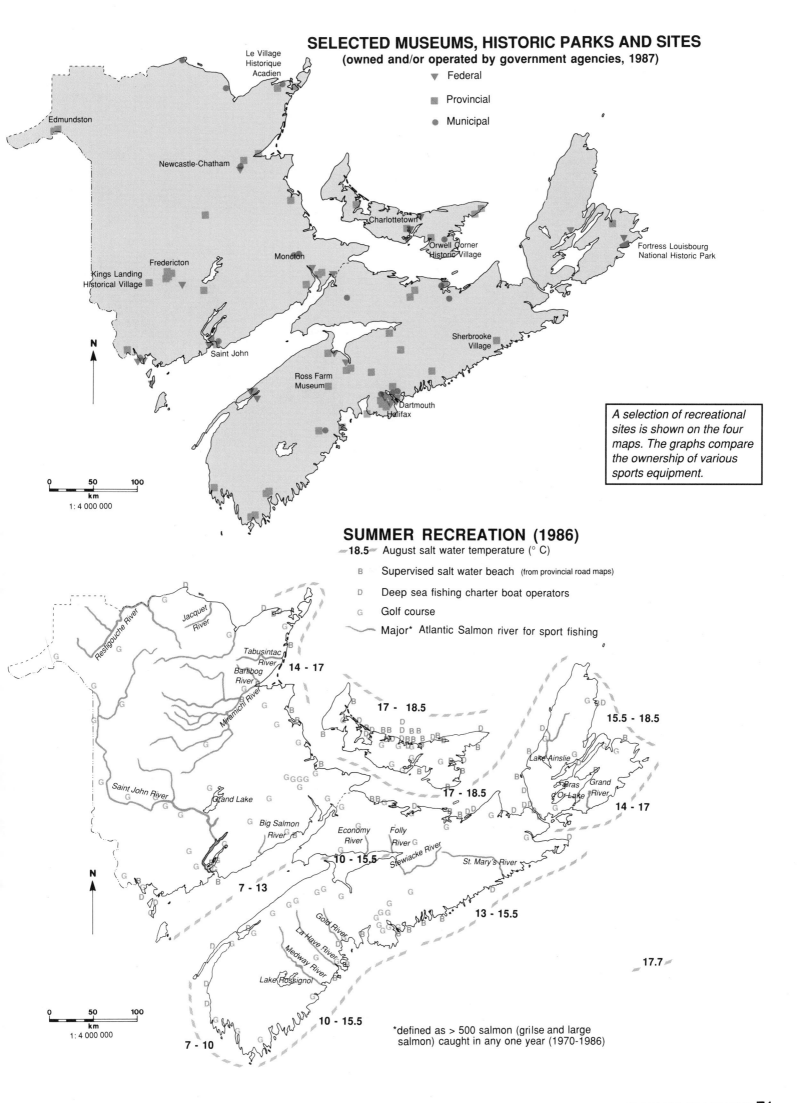

SELECTED MUSEUMS, HISTORIC PARKS AND SITES
(owned and/or operated by government agencies, 1987)

▼ Federal

■ Provincial

● Municipal

Le Village Historique Acadien

Edmundston

Newcastle-Chatham

Fredericton

Kings Landing Historical Village

Moncton

Charlottetown

Orwell Corner Historic Village

Fortress Louisbourg National Historic Park

Sherbrooke Village

Saint John

Ross Farm Museum

Dartmouth
Halifax

N

| 0 | 50 | 100 |

km

1: 4 000 000

A selection of recreational sites is shown on the four maps. The graphs compare the ownership of various sports equipment.

SUMMER RECREATION (1986)

18.5 August salt water temperature (° C)

B   Supervised salt water beach (from provincial road maps)

D   Deep sea fishing charter boat operators

G   Golf course

Major* Atlantic Salmon river for sport fishing

Jacquet River

Restigouche River

Tabusintac River

Bartibog River

Miramichi River

14 - 17

17 - 18.5

15.5 - 18.5

Lake Ainslie

Saint John River

Grand Lake

Bras d'Or Lake

Grand River

17 - 18.5

14 - 17

Big Salmon River

Economy River

Folly River

Stewiacke River

St. Mary's River

10 - 15.5

7 - 13

13 - 15.5

Gold River

La Have River

Medway River

Lake Rossignol

17.7

10 - 15.5

7 - 10

*defined as > 500 salmon (grilse and large salmon) caught in any one year (1970-1986)

N

| 0 | 50 | 100 |

km

1: 4 000 000

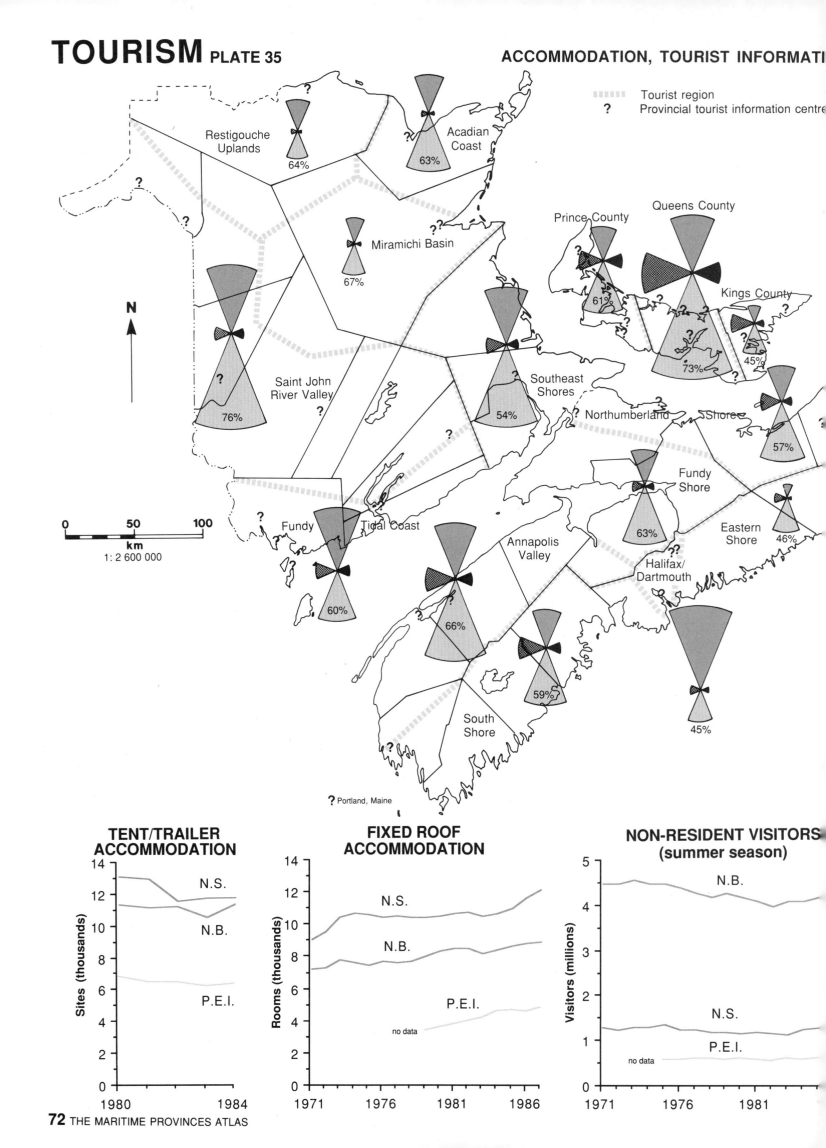

▪▪▪▪▪▪ Tourist region
? Provincial tourist information centre

Restigouche Uplands
64%

Acadian Coast
63%

Miramichi Basin
67%

Saint John River Valley
76%

Prince County
61%

Queens County
73%

Kings County
45%

Southeast Shores
54%

Northumberland Shore
57%

Fundy Shore
63%

Eastern Shore
46%

Fundy Tidal Coast
60%

Annapolis Valley
66%

Halifax/Dartmouth
45%

South Shore
59%

N

0   50   100
km
1: 2 600 000

? Portland, Maine

TENT/TRAILER ACCOMMODATION

Sites (thousands)

N.S.
N.B.
P.E.I.

14
12
10
8
6
4
2
0

1980   1984

FIXED ROOF ACCOMMODATION

Rooms (thousands)

N.S.
N.B.
P.E.I.
no data

14
12
10
8
6
4
2
0

1971   1976   1981   1986

NON-RESIDENT VISITORS
(summer season)

Visitors (millions)

N.B.
N.S.
P.E.I.
no data

5
4
3
2
1
0

1971   1976   1981

TRAVEL INDUSTRY JOBS* GENERATED BY TOURISM (1986)

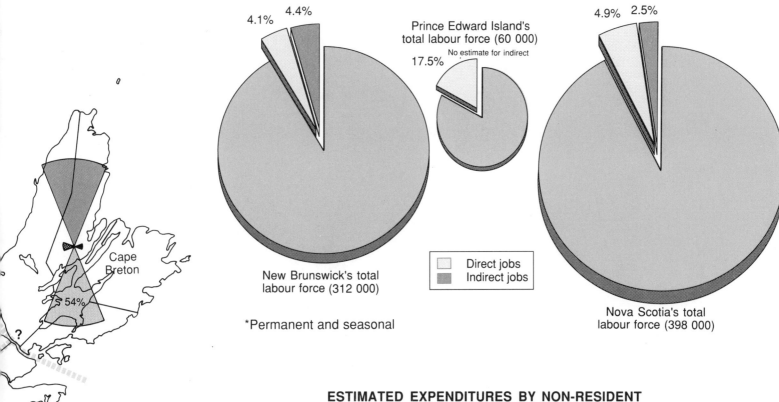

4.1% 4.4%

Prince Edward Island's total labour force (60 000)

No estimate for indirect

17.5%

New Brunswick's total labour force (312 000)

4.9% 2.5%

Direct jobs
Indirect jobs

Nova Scotia's total labour force (398 000)

*Permanent and seasonal

Cape Breton

≤ 54%

?

Type of accommodation

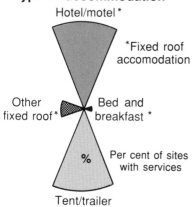

Hotel/motel*

*Fixed roof accomodation

Other fixed roof*   Bed and breakfast *

%   Per cent of sites with services

Tent/trailer

Number of rooms or campsites by tourist region

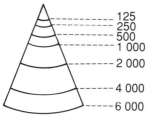

125
250
500
1 000
2 000
4 000
6 000

ESTIMATED EXPENDITURES BY NON-RESIDENT OVERNIGHT TOURISTS

	N.B.(1983)	N.S.(1986)	P.E.I.(1985)
Total auto visitors	1 343 000	769 000	520 000
Total expenditures	$120 600 000	$96 000 000	$53 000 000
Average expenditure per person	$90	$125	$102

The main map indicates the amount and type of accommodation in each tourist region. Changes in available space and number of visitors are in line graphs (bottom left). The pie graphs and table (above) indicate jobs created and money spent by tourists. Where the tourists travel from is shown for each province (below).

ORIGIN OF TOURISTS TRAVELLING BY AUTOMOBILE

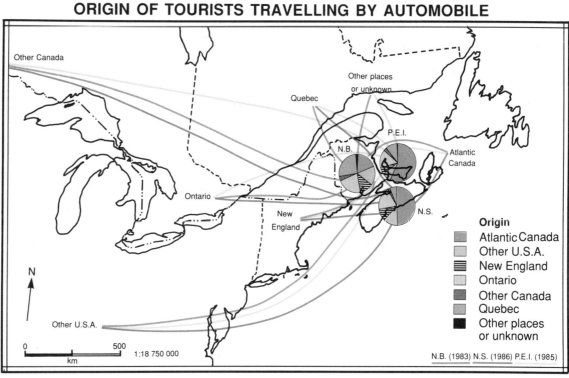

Other Canada
Quebec
Other places or unknown
P.E.I.
N.B.
Atlantic Canada
Ontario
New England
N.S.
Other U.S.A.

N

0 500 km   1:18 750 000

Origin
Atlantic Canada
Other U.S.A.
New England
Ontario
Other Canada
Quebec
Other places or unknown

N.B. (1983) N.S. (1986) P.E.I. (1985)

ROAD TRANSPORTATION PLATE 36

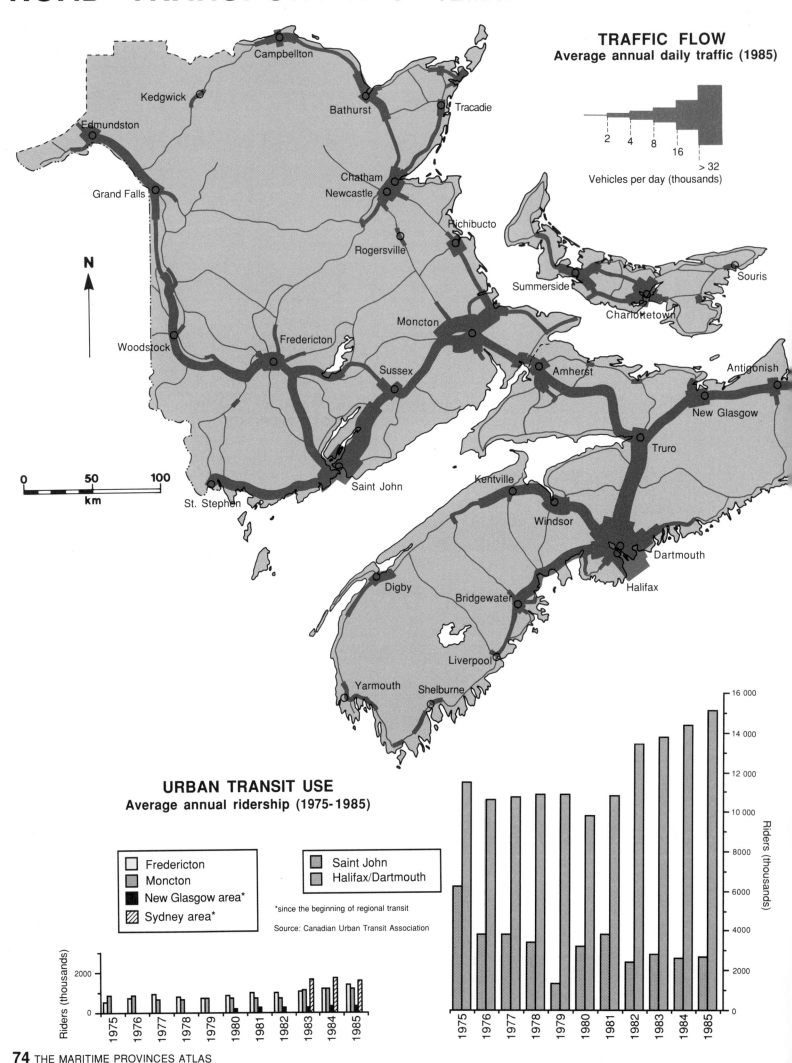

TRAFFIC FLOW
Average annual daily traffic (1985)

2   4   8   16   > 32

Vehicles per day (thousands)

N

Campbellton
Kedgwick
Edmundston
Bathurst
Tracadie
Grand Falls
Chatham
Newcastle
Richibucto
Rogersville
Summerside
Souris
Charlottetown
Moncton
Woodstock
Fredericton
Sussex
Amherst
Antigonish
New Glasgow
Truro
Saint John
Kentville
St. Stephen
Windsor
Dartmouth
Digby
Halifax
Bridgewater
Liverpool
Yarmouth
Shelburne

0   50   100
km

URBAN TRANSIT USE
Average annual ridership (1975-1985)

Riders (thousands)

| Fredericton |
| Moncton |
| New Glasgow area* |
| Sydney area* |

| Saint John |
| Halifax/Dartmouth |

*since the beginning of regional transit

Source: Canadian Urban Transit Association

Riders (thousands)

16 000
14 000
12 000
10 000
8000
6000
4000
2000
0

1975 1976 1977 1978 1979 1980 1981 1982 1983 1984 1985

2000
0
1975 1976 1977 1978 1979 1980 1981 1982 1983 1984 1985

The map shows the number of vehicles counted on each highway on an average day. The number of people using urban buses is shown in the graph below. Intercity buses offer a large number of destinations (right). The freight moved by major trucking firms is shown lower right.

INTERCITY BUS NETWORK (1986)

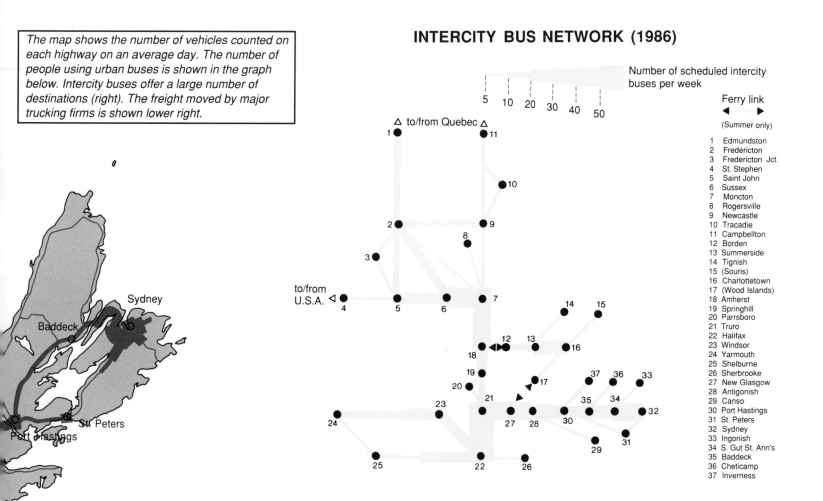

Number of scheduled intercity buses per week

5 10 20 30 40 50

Ferry link

◄ — — — ►

(Summer only)

1 Edmundston
2 Fredericton
3 Fredericton Jct.
4 St. Stephen
5 Saint John
6 Sussex
7 Moncton
8 Rogersville
9 Newcastle
10 Tracadie
11 Campbellton
12 Borden
13 Summerside
14 Tignish
15 (Souris)
16 Charlottetown
17 (Wood Islands)
18 Amherst
19 Springhill
20 Parrsboro
21 Truro
22 Halifax
23 Windsor
24 Yarmouth
25 Shelburne
26 Sherbrooke
27 New Glasgow
28 Antigonish
29 Canso
30 Port Hastings
31 St. Peters
32 Sydney
33 Ingonish
34 S. Gut St. Ann's
35 Baddeck
36 Cheticamp
37 Inverness

FOR-HIRE TRUCKING FREIGHT FLOW (1983)*

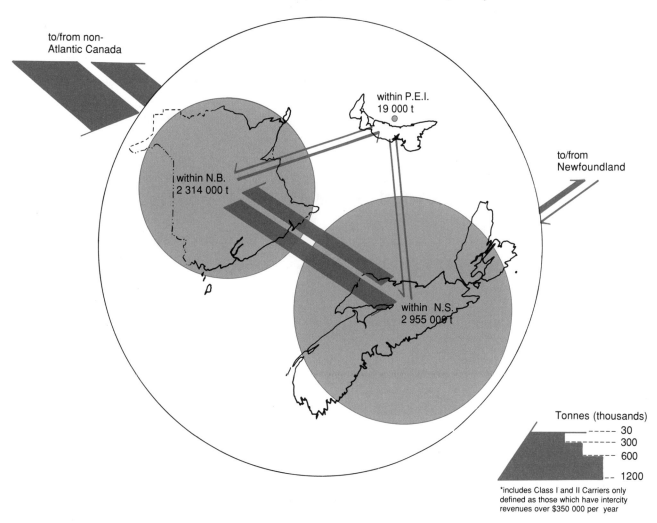

to/from non-Atlantic Canada

within P.E.I. 19 000 t

to/from Newfoundland

within N.B. 2 314 000 t

within N.S. 2 955 000 t

Tonnes (thousands)

30
300
600
1200

*includes Class I and II Carriers only defined as those which have intercity revenues over $350 000 per year

RAIL AND WATER TRANSPORTATION PLATE 37

MAJOR PORTS, RAILROADS AND FERRY LINKS

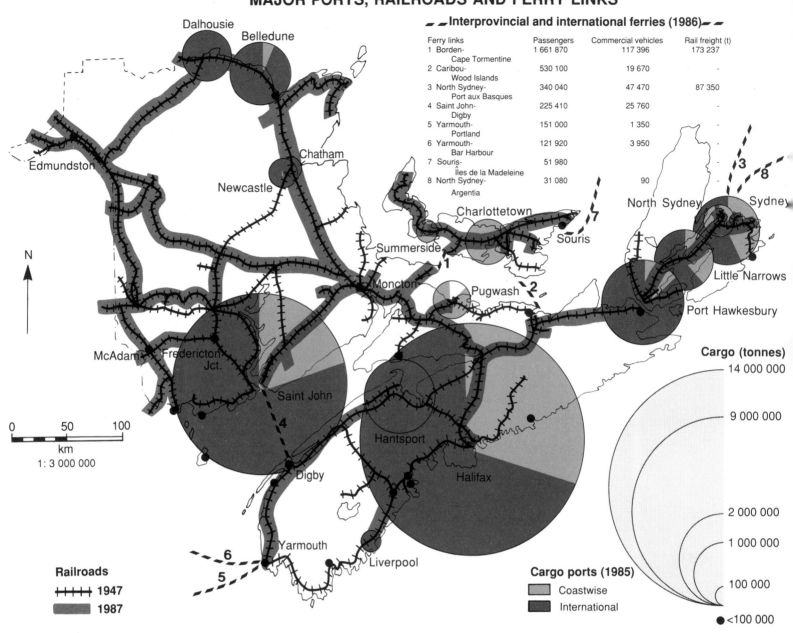

Interprovincial and international ferries (1986)

Ferry links	Passengers	Commercial vehicles	Rail freight (t)
1 Borden-Cape Tormentine	1 661 870	117 396	173 237
2 Caribou-Wood Islands	530 100	19 670	-
3 North Sydney-Port aux Basques	340 040	47 470	87 350
4 Saint John-Digby	225 410	25 760	-
5 Yarmouth-Portland	151 000	1 350	-
6 Yarmouth-Bar Harbour	121 920	3 950	-
7 Souris-Îles de la Madeleine	51 980	-	-
8 North Sydney-Argentia	31 080	90	-

Cargo (tonnes)

14 000 000
9 000 000
2 000 000
1 000 000
100 000
● <100 000

Railroads

+++++ 1947

▬ 1987

Cargo ports (1985)

Coastwise
International

COASTWISE SHIPPING FROM HALIFAX AND SAINT JOHN

1961

Halifax
Saint John

1982

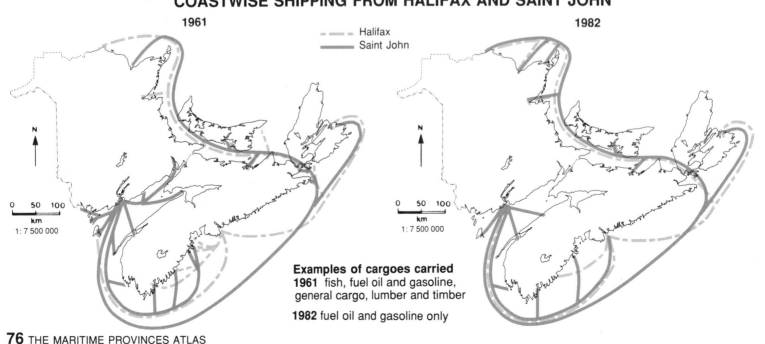

Examples of cargoes carried

1961 fish, fuel oil and gasoline, general cargo, lumber and timber

1982 fuel oil and gasoline only

RAIL PASSENGER NETWORKS

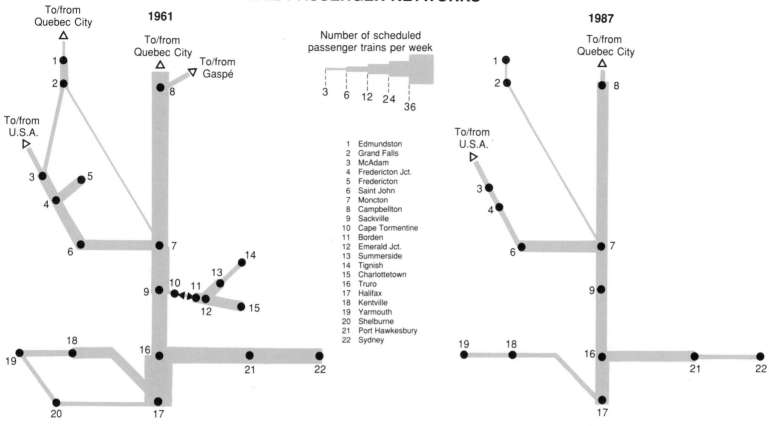

1961

To/from Quebec City

To/from Quebec City

To/from Gaspé

To/from U.S.A.

Number of scheduled passenger trains per week

3 6 12 24 36

1 Edmundston
2 Grand Falls
3 McAdam
4 Fredericton Jct.
5 Fredericton
6 Saint John
7 Moncton
8 Campbellton
9 Sackville
10 Cape Tormentine
11 Borden
12 Emerald Jct.
13 Summerside
14 Tignish
15 Charlottetown
16 Truro
17 Halifax
18 Kentville
19 Yarmouth
20 Shelburne
21 Port Hawkesbury
22 Sydney

1987

To/from Quebec City

To/from U.S.A.

The main map and diagrams (above) indicate the shrinking rail network. Details of water transportation are provided with ports and ferries shown on the map, a table of ferry operations (top left) and maps of coastal cargo movements (bottom left). The graphs (below) further highlight the changes in rail and water freight transportation.

WATER FREIGHT

COASTWISE

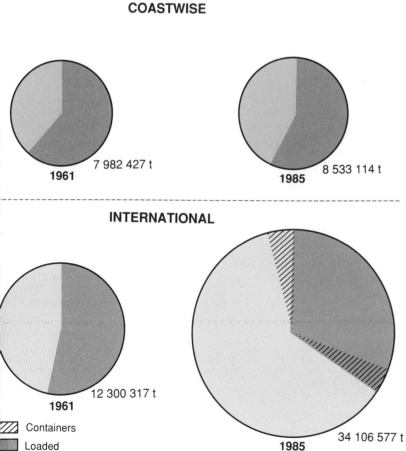

1961 7 982 427 t

1985 8 533 114 t

INTERNATIONAL

1961 12 300 317 t

1985 34 106 577 t

Containers
Loaded
Unloaded

RAIL FREIGHT

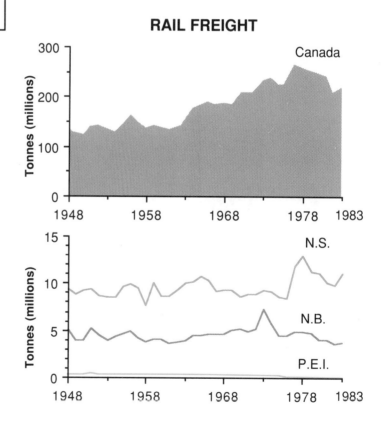

Canada

N.S.

N.B.

P.E.I.

AIR TRANSPORTATION PLATE 38

AIR PASSENGER NETWORK (1987)

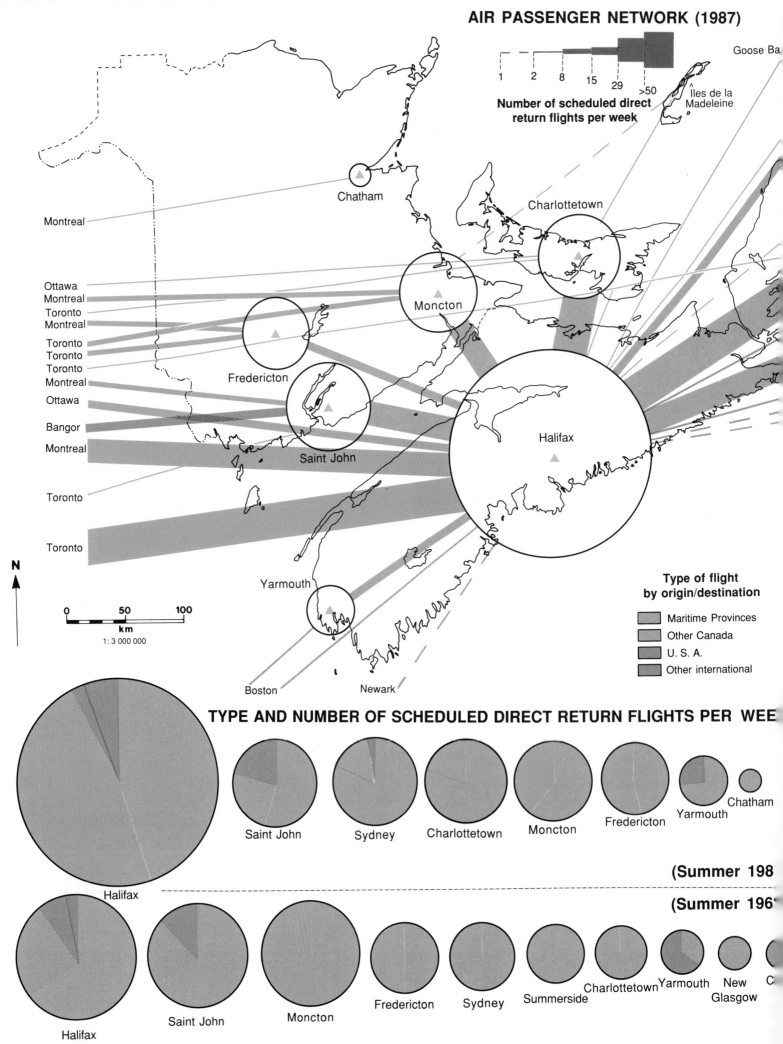

Number of scheduled direct return flights per week

1 2 8 15 29 >50

Goose Ba

Îles de la Madeleine

Chatham

Charlottetown

Montreal

Ottawa
Montreal
Toronto
Montreal
Toronto
Toronto
Toronto
Montreal
Ottawa
Bangor
Montreal

Toronto

Toronto

Moncton

Fredericton

Saint John

Halifax

N

0   50   100
km
1 : 3 000 000

Yarmouth

Boston   Newark

Type of flight by origin/destination

Maritime Provinces
Other Canada
U. S. A.
Other international

TYPE AND NUMBER OF SCHEDULED DIRECT RETURN FLIGHTS PER WEE

Halifax

Saint John   Sydney   Charlottetown   Moncton   Fredericton   Yarmouth   Chatham

(Summer 198

(Summer 196

Halifax   Saint John   Moncton   Fredericton   Sydney   Summerside   Charlottetown   Yarmouth   New Glasgow   C

78 THE MARITIME PROVINCES ATLAS

AIR TRAFFIC CONTROL ZONES AT SELECTED AIRPORTS (1987)

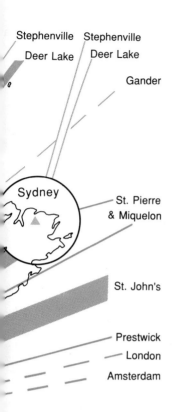

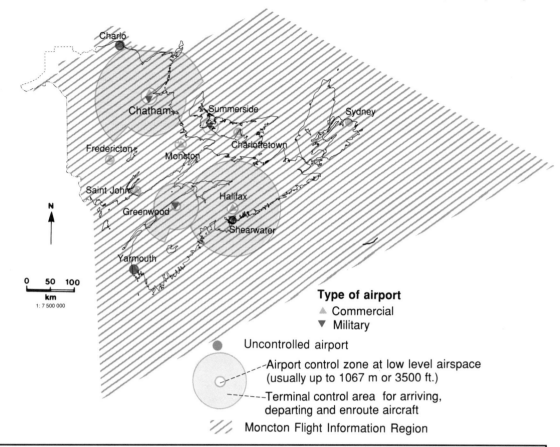

Type of airport
- ▲ Commercial
- ▼ Military

- ● Uncontrolled airport
- Airport control zone at low level airspace (usually up to 1067 m or 3500 ft.)
- Terminal control area for arriving, departing and enroute aircraft
- /// Moncton Flight Information Region

The main map shows the commercial airports and the number of flights between them and other important destinations. The pie graphs show the changes in the flights to and from airports in the Maritimes. The map (above) depicts different air traffic control zones. The line graphs (below) illustrate the growth of air freight and passengers.

Number of scheduled direct return flights per week

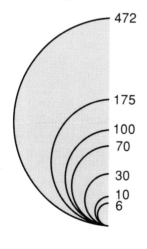

- 472
- 175
- 100
- 70
- 30
- 10
- 6

AIR FREIGHT AT THE HALIFAX INTERNATIONAL AIRPORT

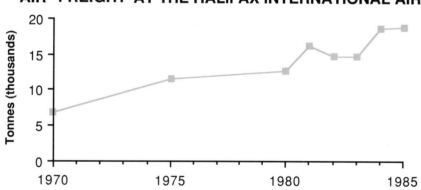

PASSENGER TRAFFIC AT SELECTED AIRPORTS (1968-1985)

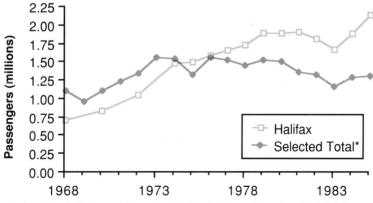

Legend:
- □ Halifax
- ◆ Selected Total*

* Includes Charlottetown (since 1975), Fredericton, Moncton, Saint John, and Sydney.

COMMUNICATIONS PLATE 39

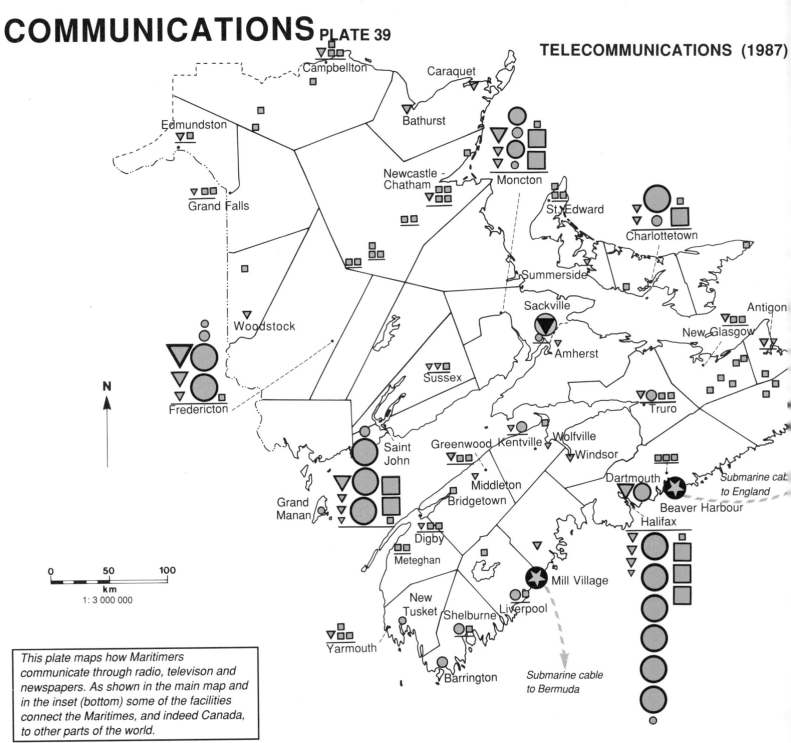

Campbellton
Caraquet
Edmundston
Bathurst
Newcastle - Chatham
Grand Falls
Moncton
St. Edward
Charlottetown
Woodstock
Summerside
Sackville
Antigon
New Glasgow
Fredericton
Amherst
Sussex
Truro
Saint John
Greenwood Kentville Wolfville
Windsor
Dartmouth
Submarine cab
to England
Grand Manan
Middleton
Bridgetown
Beaver Harbour
Digby
Halifax
Meteghan
Mill Village
New Tusket
Shelburne Liverpool
Submarine cable
to Bermuda
Yarmouth
Barrington

N

0   50   100
km
1 : 3 000 000

This plate maps how Maritimers communicate through radio, televison and newspapers. As shown in the main map and in the inset (bottom) some of the facilities connect the Maritimes, and indeed Canada, to other parts of the world.

CABLE TELEVISION (1986)

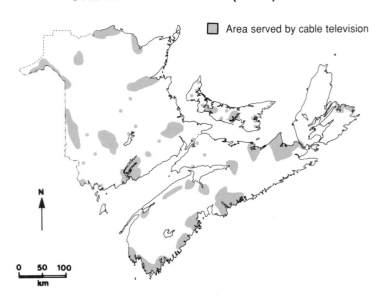

■ Area served by cable television

N

0 50 100
km

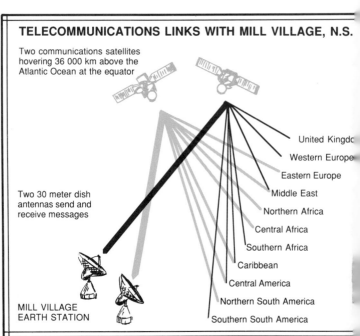

TELECOMMUNICATIONS LINKS WITH MILL VILLAGE, N.S.

Two communications satellites hovering 36 000 km above the Atlantic Ocean at the equator

Two 30 meter dish antennas send and receive messages

MILL VILLAGE
EARTH STATION

United Kingdo
Western Europe
Eastern Europe
Middle East
Northern Africa
Central Africa
Southern Africa
Caribbean
Central America
Northern South America
Southern South America

DAILY NEWSPAPERS (1988)

Caraquet

Summerside
Charlottetown
Sydney

Fredericton
Moncton
Amherst
New Glasgow
Saint John
Truro
Dartmouth

Halifax

N

0   50   100
km

Names of the Daily Newspapers

Caraquet	L'Acadie Nouvelle
Fredericton	Daily Gleaner
Moncton	Le Matin
	The Times-Transcript
Saint John	Telegraph-Journal
	Evening Times Globe
Amherst	Daily News
Dartmouth	The Daily News
Halifax	The Chronicle-Herald
	The Mail Star
New Glasgow	The Evening News
Sydney	Cape Breton Post
Truro	The Daily News
Charlottetown	Guardian
	Patriot
Summerside	Journal Pioneer

Language
- English
- French

Television stations
- ☐ Broadcast station
- ▫ Rebroadcast station

AM FM Radio stations
- ▽ ◯ 100 000 watts
- ▽ ◯ 50 000 - 99 999 watts
- ▽ ◦ 5 000 - 49 999 watts
- ▽ ◦ < 5 000 watts
- ⬤ Radio Canada International Shortwave Transmitting Station
- ✪ Telecommunications site

Language
- English
- French
- Both

Circulation
- ▫ < 2 500
- ◻ 2 500 - 4 999
- ☐ 5 000 - 9 999
- ☐ 10 000 - 24 999
- ☐ 25 000 - 50 000
- ☐ > 50 000

(ness)
(Sydney)
(Port Hawkesbury)

WEEKLY NEWSPAPERS (1988)

Dalhousie
Campbellton
Caraquet

Bathurst

Edmundston

Newcastle
Grand Falls
Chatham
Richibucto
Alberton
Inverness

Perth-Andover
Shediac
Summerside
Montague

Hartland
Woodstock
Sackville
Amherst
Oxford
Pictou
Antigonish
Port Hawkesbury

Oromocto
Sussex
Springhill
Truro

Kentville
St. Stephen
Windsor
Middleton
Berwick
Enfield
Saint John
Bridgetown
Greenwood
Bedford
Digby
Annapolis Royal
Cornwallis

Liverpool
Bridgewater

Yarmouth
Shelburne

N

0   50   100
km

EXPORTS (1986)

Value $ (millions)

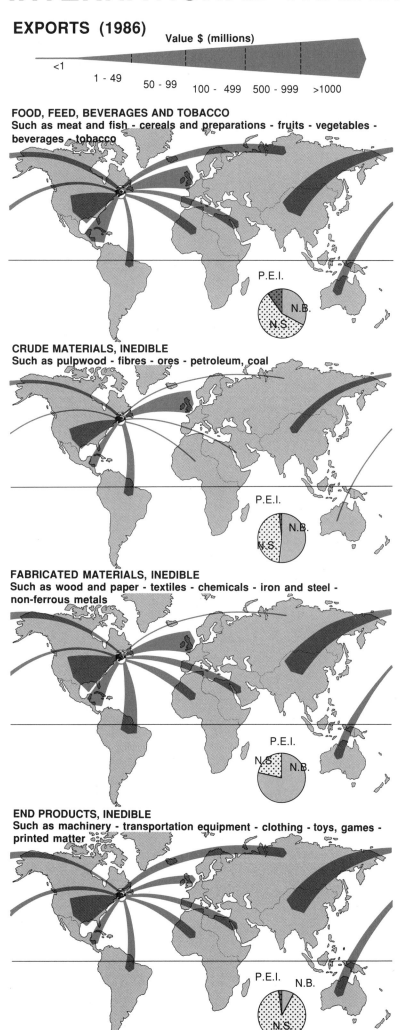

<1	1 - 49	50 - 99	100 - 499	500 - 999	>1000

FOOD, FEED, BEVERAGES AND TOBACCO
Such as meat and fish - cereals and preparations - fruits - vegetables - beverages - tobacco

P.E.I.
N.B.
N.S.

CRUDE MATERIALS, INEDIBLE
Such as pulpwood - fibres - ores - petroleum, coal

P.E.I.
N.B.
N.S.

FABRICATED MATERIALS, INEDIBLE
Such as wood and paper - textiles - chemicals - iron and steel - non-ferrous metals

P.E.I.
N.S.
N.B.

END PRODUCTS, INEDIBLE
Such as machinery - transportation equipment - clothing - toys, games - printed matter

P.E.I.
N.B.
N.S.

TOTAL EXPORTS TO WORLD REGIONS F

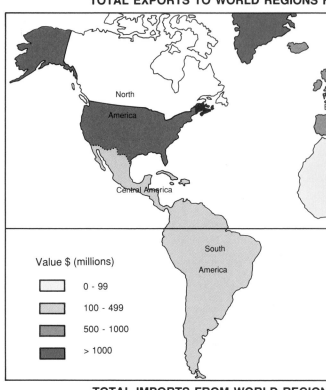

Value $ (millions)

	0 - 99
	100 - 499
	500 - 1000
	> 1000

TOTAL IMPORTS FROM WORLD REGION

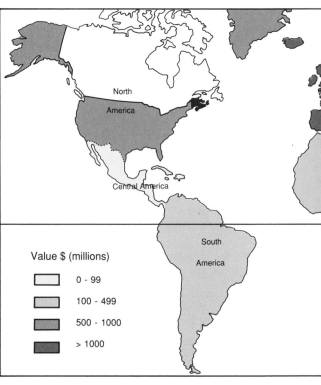

Value $ (millions)

	0 - 99
	100 - 499
	500 - 1000
	> 1000

TRADE OF THE MARITIME PROVINCES

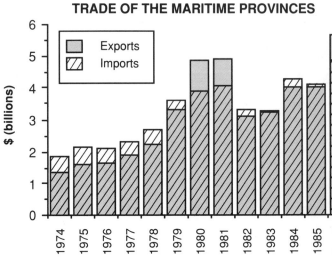

Exports
Imports

$ (billions)

1974 1975 1976 1977 1978 1979 1980 1981 1982 1983 1984 1985

MARITIME PROVINCES (1986)

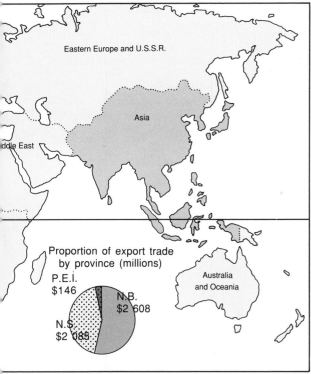

Eastern Europe and U.S.S.R.

Asia

Middle East

Australia and Oceania

Proportion of export trade by province (millions)
P.E.I. $146
N.B. $2 608
N.S. $2 085

MARITIME PROVINCES (1986)

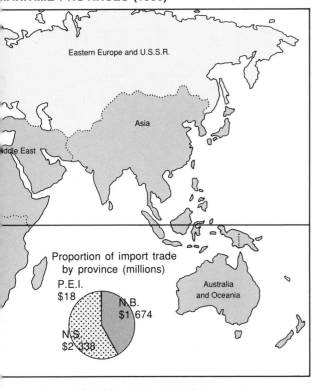

Eastern Europe and U.S.S.R.

Asia

Middle East

Australia and Oceania

Proportion of import trade by province (millions)
P.E.I. $18
N.B. $1 674
N.S. $2 338

TOP EXPORTS AND IMPORTS (1986)

EXPORTS		IMPORTS	
607 887 770		N.B. $1 673 810 390	
d pulp	$572 813 500	1. Crude petroleum	$774 127 135
sprint paper	$375 335 729	2. Fuel oil	$124 222 000
ricity	$276 694 395	3. Raw sugar	$50 120 946
oil	$231 986 400	4. Rubber tire fabrics	$27 524 548
line	$174 449 276	5. Paper for printing	$21 371 334
084 908 063		N.S. $2 338 423 113	
for motor vehicles	$359 702 300	1. Automobiles; new	$774 474 400
sprint paper	$226 397 679	2. Crude petroleum	$669 034 966
fresh, frozen, salted	$180 341 700	3. Fuel oil	$102 784 700
d pulp	$177 820 400	4. Auto parts, accessories	$89 565 172
ters and lobster meat	$129 352 400	5. Frozen boneless beef	$60 163 049
46 194 735		P.E.I. $17 659 541	
toes; fresh and seed	$36 515 778	1. Eyeglasses and frame parts	$3 754 076
ter meat; fresh, frozen	$26 182 493	2. Urea	$1 762 498
to products; frozen	$17 680 567	3. Potassic fertilizer	$1 141 838
ronic computers, parts	$8 383 313	4. Electronic computers, parts	$1 028 957
evaporated	$ 7 783 140	5. Fuel oil	$754 402

nd export figures represent province of entry and province of departure respectively. Imports,
, do not necessarily remain in the province. For example, automobiles are destined primarily for
in Ontario and Quebec. As far as is known, exports are products of the Maritime Provinces.

IMPORTS (1986)

Value $ (millions)
>1000   500 - 999   100 - 499   50 - 99   1 - 49   <1

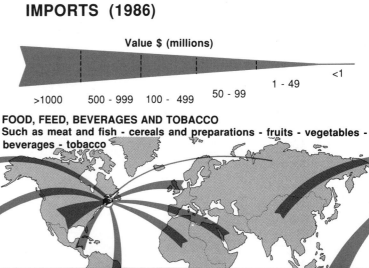

FOOD, FEED, BEVERAGES AND TOBACCO
Such as meat and fish - cereals and preparations - fruits - vegetables - beverages - tobacco

P.E.I.
N.S.   N.B.

CRUDE MATERIALS, INEDIBLE
Such as pulpwood - fibres - ores - petroleum, coal

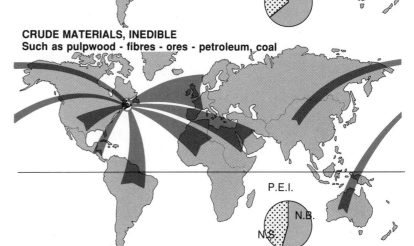

P.E.I.
N.B.
N.S.

FABRICATED MATERIALS, INEDIBLE
Such as wood and paper - textiles - chemicals - iron and steel - non-ferrous metals

P.E.I.
N.B.
N.S.

END PRODUCTS, INEDIBLE
Such as machinery - transportation equipment - clothing - toys, games - printed matter

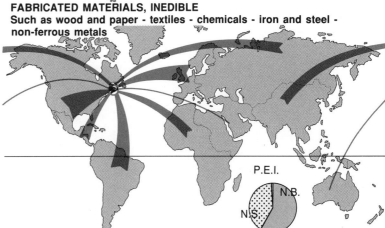

P.E.I.
N.B.
N.S.

GAZETTEER

GAZETTEER LAYOUT

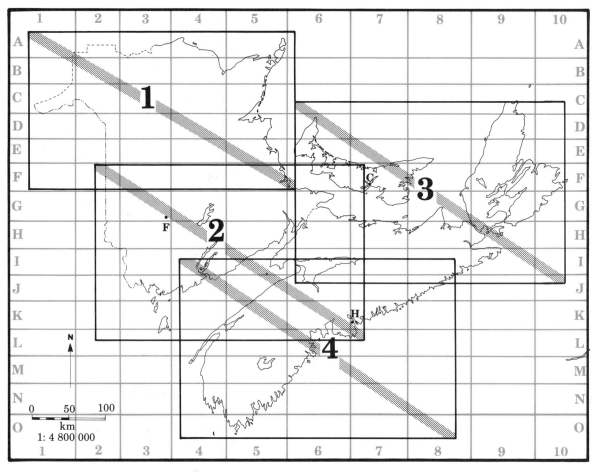

EXAMPLE C- Charlottetown ... F7 (Row F, Column 7), **F-**Fredericton ... G3, **H-**Halifax ... K7

GAZETTEER MAP SYMBOLS

Trans Canada Highway *Route transcanadienne*	Railway *Chemin de fer*	Boat Slip/Launch *Rampe de mise à l'eau*
Provincial Arterial *Artère provinciale*	Ferry *Traversier*	Marina and/or Boating Excursions *Marina et (ou) excursions en bateau*
Trunk Highway *Grand-route*	Coastal Boat *Bateau côtier*	Canoe Routes *Routes pour canots*
Collector Road *Route collectrice*	Customs/Border Crossing *Douane/Frontière*	Non-supervised Beach *Plage non-surveillée*
Local Road *Route locale*	M.O.T. Airport *Aéroport Transports Canada*	Supervised Beach *Plage surveillée*
Paved, Unpaved *Asphaltée, non asphaltée*	Small Airport *Aéroport secondaire*	Picnic Area (Day Use Prov. Park) *Terrain de pique-nique (Parc prov. d'utilisation diurne)*
Prince Edward Island Scenic Drives *Routes panoramiques de l'I.-P.-É.*	Lighthouse *Phare*	**Campground** *Terrain de camping*
- Lady Slipper Drive - *Promenade Lady Slipper*	Provincial Boundary *Frontière provinciale*	- Federal - *Fédéral*
- Blue Heron Drive - *Promenade Blue Heron*	International Boundary *Frontière internationale*	- Provincial - *Provincial*
- Kings Byway - *Chemin du Roi*	Tourist Region Boundary *Limite de région touristique*	- Other - *Autres*
Nova Scotia Travelways *Voies de circulation en Nouvelle-Ecosse*	Hospital *Hôpital*	**Tourist Information Centre** *Centre d'information touristique*
- Lighthouse Route - *Route du phare*	National or Provincial Park *Parc national ou provincial*	- Provincial - *Provincial*
- Evangeline Trail - *Piste Evangéline*	Game santuary/Wilderness Area *Réserve de gibier/Zone vierge*	- Other - *Autres*
- Glooscap Trail - *Piste Glooscap*	Alpine Skiing *Ski alpin*	Golf Course *Terrain de golf*
- Sunrise Trail - *Piste de lever du soleil*	Cross Country Skiing *Ski de fond*	- Theatre - *Théâtre*
- Cabot Trail - *Piste Cabot*	Hiking Trail *Sentier de randonnage*	- Museum - *Musée*
- Fleur-de-lis-Trail - *Piste Fleur-de-lis*	Significant Natural Areas *Zones naturelles intéressantes*	- Historic Site - *Lieu historique*
- Marine Drive - *Promenade côtière*	**Sports Fishing** *Pêche sportive*	
- Celidh Trail - *Piste Celidh*	- Rod - *Pêche à la ligne*	
- Halifax - Dartmouth Metro - *Métropole Halifax - Dartmouth*	- Tuna - *Pêche au thon*	
	- Deep Sea - *Pêche hauturière*	

The gazetteer maps are based upon the Maritime Resource Management Service *Atlantic Canada Vacation Guide Map*, 2nd edition, 1987

NEW BRUNSWICK

Place	Grid	Place	Grid
…adieville	E5	Nashwaak Bridge	F3
…msville	F5	Neguac	C5
…suane	E5	Nelson-Miramichi	D5
…rdville	B5	New Denmark	D2
…la	H5	Newcastle	D5
…gance	H5	Nicolas Dénys	B4
…haqui	H5	Nictau	C3
…stook Junction	E2	Nigadoo	B4
…urette	E3	Norton	H4
…alville	A3	Notre-Dame	F5
…ac	G6	Oromocto	H4
…-Ste-Anne	D5	Ortonville	D2
… Verte	G6	Paquetville	B5
…er Brook	C1	Pennefield Corner	J3
…noral	A3	Penobsquis	H5
…aby River	D5	Perth-Andover	E2
…bog Bridge	D5	Petit-Cap	F6
…	F2	Petit-Rocher	A4
…urst	B4	Petitcodiac	G5
…urst Mines	C4	Petite-Rivière-de-d'Ile	A5
… du Vin	D5	Plaster Rock	D3
…ield	G6	Pointe-Sapin	D5
…er Brook Sta.	D4	Pointe-Verte	A4
…edune	A4	Pokemouche	B5
… Lomond	I4	Pokiok	G3
…ton	G2	Port Elgin	G6
…esford	B4	Prince William	H3
…rand	B5	Quarryville	D4
…vick	H5	Queenstown	H4
…ks Harbour	J3	Quispamsis	I4
…kville	E4	Red Bank	D4
…stown	F4	Renforth	I4
…ol	C5	Renous	E4
…ol	F2	Rexton	E5
…kway	I3	Richibucto	E5
…son Settlement	F4	Richibucto Village	E5
…wns Flat	I4	River de Chute	E2
…ctouche	F5	River Glade	G5
…ts Corner	G3	Riverside-Albert	H5
…bridge	H4	Riverview	G5
…pbellton	A3	Rivière-Verte	C2
…aan Station	F5	Rivière-du-Portage	B5
…erbury Station	H3	Robertville	B4
…-Pelé	F6	Robinsonville	A3
…e Tormentine	G6	Rockport	H6
…aquet	A5	Rogersville	E5
…treville	F2	Rosaireville	E5
…rlo	A4	Rothesay	I4
…tham	D5	Sackville	G6
…tham Head	D5	Saint John	I4
…man	G4	Saint-Paul	F5
…	C1	Salisbury	G5
… Branch Station	F6	Shediac	F6
…agne	G4	Sheila	B5
…s Island	G4	Shippagan	B5
…ge Bridge	G6	Silverwood	G3
…ette	E5	St-André	D2
…berland Bay	G4	St. Andrews	J3
…ousie	A4	St-Anselme	G5
…sonville	A3	St-Antoine	E5
…pe	G5	St-Basile	C2
…eguash	J3	St-Edouard-de-Kent	E5
…ktown	E4	St-Francois-de-Madawaska	C1
…ktown	G6	St. George	J3
…hester Crossing	F5	St-Hilaire	C1
…glastown	D5	St-Ignace	E5
…nmond	D2	St-Isidore	B5
…afries	G3	St-Jacques	C1
…uis Corner	F6	St-Jean Baptiste-de-Restigouche	B3
…ham Bridge	G4	St-Joseph	G6
…undston	C2	St-Léolin	B5
… River Crossing	A4	St-Léonard	D2
…n	H5	St-Louis-de-Kent	E5
…ndale	H4	St. Margarets	D5
…vale	I4	St. Martins	I5
…enceville	F2	St-Quentin	B3
…ericton	G3	St-Raphael-sur-Mer	B5
…ericton Junction	H3	St-Sauveur	B5
…etown	H4	St-Simon	B5
…ry	H4	St. Stephen	J3
…dola Point	I4	Stanley	F3
…d Bay	I4	Ste-Anne-de-Kent	E5
…d Falls	D2	Ste-Anne-de-Madawaska	C2
…d Harbour	K3	Ste-Marie-de-Kent	F5
…de-Anse	A5	Ste-Rose	B5
…de-Digue	F6	Stickney	F2
…pton	I4	Sunny Corner	D4
…t	F5	Sussex	H5
…land	F3	Sussex Corner	H5
…rey	H5	Tabusintac	C5
…rey Station	H3	Taymouth	G4
…eld Point	H4	Thomaston Corner	H3
…te Aboujagane	G6	Tide Head	A3
…elock	G5	Tracadie	B5
…borough	G5	Tracy	H3
…ewell Cape	H6	Upper Blackville	E4
…ard	E4	Verret	C1
…rman	B5	Village Acadien	B5
…quet River	A4	Welsford	I4
…ure	G6	Westfield	I4
…oer	E3	Whites Brook	B3
…gwick	B3	Woodstock	G2
… Junction	E5	Youngs Cove	G4
…s Landing	H3		
…chibouguac	E5		
…Baker	C1		
…èque	A5		
…lette	C5		
…rence Station	I3		

NOVA SCOTIA

Place	Grid	Place	Grid	Place	Grid	Place	Grid	Place	Grid
Advocate Harbour	I5	Ballantynes Cove	G8	Glace Bay	F10	Martock	J6	Sandy Point	N5
Albany Cross	K5	Barachois	F9	Glen Margaret	K6	Maryville	G8	Saulnierville	M4
Aldershot	J6	Barrington	O5	Glendale	G9	Masstown	I7	Scotch Village	J6
Allendale	N5	Barrington Passage	O5	Glenelg	I8	Mavillette	M4	Scotchtown	F10
Alton	J7	Barton	L4	Glenholm	I7	Meaghers Grant	J7	Scots Bay	I6
Amherst	H6	Bass River	I6	Goldboro	I8	Meat Cove	C9	Scotsburn	H7
Annapolis Royal	K5	Baxter's Harbour	I6	Goldenville	J8	Medway	M6	Scotsville	F9
Antigonish	H8	Bay St. Lawrence	C9	Gore	J6	Melford	H9	Seabright	K6
Apple River	I5	Bear Cove	M4	Goshen	I8	Melrose	I8	Seafoam	H7
Arcadie	N4	Bear River	L5	Grand Etang	E9	Merigomish	H8	Seaforth	K7
Argyle	N4	Beaver River	M4	Grand Lake	J7	Meteghan	M4	Seal Harbour	I8
Arichat	H9	Beaverbank	K6	Grand Narrows	G9	Meteghan River	M4	Selma	I7
Arisaig	H8	Bedford	K6	Grand Pré	J6	Middle Clyde River	N5	Shad Bay	L6
Aspen	I8	Belle Côte	E9	Grande Anse	H9	Middle Musquodoboit	J7	Shag Harbour	O5
Auburn	J5	Belleville	N4	Great Village	I7	Middle Ohio	N5	Sheet Harbour	J8
Auld's Cove	H8	Belliveau Cove	L4	Green Oaks	I7	Middle River	F9	Shelburne	N5
Avondale	H8	Belmont	I7	Greenfield	L5	Middle Sackville	K6	Sherbrooke	I8
Avonport	J6	Ben Eoin	G9	Greenhill	H7	Middle Stewiacke	I7	Shinimicas Bridge	G6
Aylesford	J5	Berwick	J5	Greenwood	J5	Middlefield	M5	Ship Harbour	K7
Baccaro	O5	Big Bras d'Or	F9	Gulf Shore	G7	Middleton	J5	Shubenacadie	J7
Baddeck	F9	Big Harbour	F9	Gunning Cove	N5	Middlewood	M6	Shulie	H6
Bakers Settlement	L5	Big Pond	G9	Guysborough	I8	Milford	K5	Shunacadie	G9
		Birchtown	N5	Halfway Cove	I9	Milford	J7	Skir Dhu	E9
		Black Rock	I7	Halfway River	I6	Mill Village	M6	Smiths Cove	L4
		Blandford	L6	Halifax	K7	Milton	M5	Somerset	J5
		Blomidon	I6	Halls Harbour	J6	Minasville	I6	Sonora	J8
		Blue Mountain	H8	Hampton	K5	Minudie	H6	South Alton	J6
		Blue Rocks	L6	Hansford	H6	Mira	F10	South Bar	F10
		Boisdale	F9	Hantsport	J6	Mira Road	F10	South Brookfield	L5
		Boylston	H8	Harbourville	J5	Monastery	H8	South Gut St. Ann's	F9
		Bramber	J8	Hardwood Lands	J7	Moose River	I6	South Harbour	D9
		Breton Cove	E9	Harrigan Cove	J8	Moose R. Gold Mines	J7	South Maitland	I7
		Bridgetown	K5	Havelock	L4	Moosehead	J8	South Milford	L5
		Bridgeville	I7	Havre Boucher	H8	Mooseland	J7	S. W. Port Mouton	N5
		Bridgewater	L6	Hay Cove	G9	Morden	J5	Southampton	H6
		Broad Cove	M6	Hazel Hill	I9	Morristown	H8	Spencers Island	I5
		Brook Village	G9	Head of Amherst	G6	Moser River	J8	Springfield	K5
		Brookfield	I7	Head of St. Margaret's Bay	K6	Mount Uniacke	J6	Springhill	H6
		Brooklyn	M6	Heatherton	I8	Mulgrave	H8	Springhill Junction	H6
		Bucklaw	G9	Hebron	N4	Mushaboom	J8	Spry Bay	K7
		Burtons	I7	Hectanooga	M4	Musquodoboit Hbr.	K7	Spry Harbour	J7
		Caledonia	L5	Hemford	L5	Nappan	H6	St. Andrews	H8
		Caledonia	I8	Herring Cove	K7	Neil's Harbour	D9	St. Ann's	F9
		Cambridge	J6	Hilden	I7	New Cornwall	L6	St. Croix	J6
		Canning	J6	Hopewell	I7	New Germany	L5	St. Esprit	H9
		Canso	I9	Hubbards	K6	New Glasgow	H7	St. Mary's River	J8
		Cape George	G8	Hunters Mountain	F9	New Harbour	I8	St. Peters	H9
		Cape North	D9	Hunts Point	M5	New Minas	J6	St. Rose	F9
		Caribou	H7	Imperoyal	K7	New Ross	K6	Stanburn	K5
		Caribou Gold Mines	J7	Indian Brook	E9	New Salem	I5	Stanley	J6
		Caribou River	H7	Indian Harbour	L6	New Waterford	F10	Stellarton	H7
		Carleton	M4	Ingomar	O5	New Yarmouth	I5	Stewiacke	J7
		Central Grove	L4	Ingonish	D9	Newcomb Corners	J7	Stillwater	I8
		Centreville	L4	Ingonish Beach	E9	Nictaux Falls	K5	Stormont	I8
		Centreville	J6	Ingonish Ferry	E9	Nine Mile River	J7	Strathlorne	F9
		Chebogue Point	N4	Ingramport	K6	Noel	I6	Summerville	J6
		Chester	L6	Inverness	F9	North East Margaree	F9	Sutherland River	H8
		Chester Basin	L6	Iona	G9	North Grant	H8	Sydney	F10
		Chéticamp	E9	Isaacs Harbour	I8	North Shore	E9	Sydney Mines	F9
		Cheverie	J6	James River Station	H8	North Sydney	F9	Sydney River	F9
		Chezzetcook	J7	Jeddore Oyster Pond	K7	Northport	G6	Tangier	K7
		Church Point	L4	Joggins	H6	Nyanza	F9	Tantallon	K6
		Clam Harbour	K7	Jordan Bay	N5	Ogden	I8	Tatamagouche	H7
		Clarks Harbour	O5	Jordan Falls	N5	Ohio	N4	Tennycape	I6
		Clementsport	K5	Judique	G8	Orangedale	G9	Terence Bay	L6
		Clementsvale	K5	Kempt	L5	Overton	N4	The Lookoff	J6
		Cleveland	H9	Kemptown	I7	Oxford	H6	Thorburn	H7
		Clyde River	O5	Kemptville	M4	Paradise	K5	Three Mile Plains	J6
		Coddle Harbour	I8	Kennetcook	J6	Parkers Cove	K5	Tidnish	G6
		Coldbrook	J6	Kentville	J6	Parrsboro	I6	Tidnish Bridge	G6
		Collingwood Corner	H6	Ketch Harbour	L7	Peggy's Cove	L6	Timberlea	K6
		Comeau Hill	N4	Kingcross	E9	Petit Etang	E9	Tiverton	L4
		Conquerall	L6	Kingsburg	L6	Petit-de-Grat	H9	Toney River	H7
		Corberrie	M4	Kingsport	J6	Petite Rivière	M6	Tor Bay	I9
		Country Hbr. Cr. Rds.	I8	Kingston	J5	Philips Harbour	I9	Torbrook	K5
		Country Hbr. Mines	I8	Kinsmans Corners	J6	Pictou	H7	Tracadie	H8
		Craigmore	G8	L'Ardoise	H9	Pleasant Bay	D9	Trafalgar	I7
		Creignish	H8	LaHave	L6	Plympton	L4	Tremont	J5
		D'Escousse	H9	Lake Ainslie	G9	Point Cross	E9	Trenton	H7
		Dalhousie	K5	Lake George	J5	Port Bickerton	J8	Troy	H8
		Dalhousie East	K5	Lakelands	I6	Port Clyde	O5	Truemanville	G6
		Dalhousie West	K5	Lakevale	G8	Port Dufferin	J8	Truro	I7
		Dartmouth	K7	Larrys River	I9	Port George	J5	Truro Heights	I7
		Debert	I7	Lawrencetown	K5	Port Greville	I6	Tupperville	K5
		Deep Brook	K5	Lawrencetown	K7	Port Hastings	H8	Tusket	N4
		Delap Cove	K5	Liscomb	J8	Port Hood	G8	Union	I7
		Denmark	H7	Liscomb Mills	J8	Port Howe	G6	Upper Clements	K5
		Digby	L4	Lismore	H8	Port Joli	N5	Upper Economy	I6
		Dingwall	D9	Litchfield	K5	Port La Tour	O5	Upper Falmouth	J6
		Dominion	F10	Little Brook	L4	Port Lorne	J5	Upper Granville	K5
		Donkin	F10	Little Dover	I9	Port Maitland	M4	Upper Kennetcook	J6
		Doucetteville	L4	Little Narrows	G9	Port Medway	M6	Upper LaHave	L6
		Dundee	H9	Liverpool	M5	Port Morien	F10	Upper Margaree	F9
		Dunvegan	F9	Livingstone Cove	G8	Port Mouton	N5	Upper Musquodoboit	J7
		Earltown	H7	Loch Lomond	G9	Port Philip	G6	Upper Rawdon	J6
		East Bay	F9	Lochaber	I8	Port Royal	K5	Upper Sackville	K6
		East Chezzetcook	K7	Lochaber Mines	J8	Port Saxon	O5	Upper Stewiacke	I7
		East Ferry	L4	Lockeport	N8	Port Shoreham	I8	Upper Tantallon	K6
		East Jeddore	K7	Londonderry	I7	Port Williams	J6	Urbania	I7
		East Jordan	N5	Louis Head	N5	Portapique	I6	Valley	I7
		East Pubnico	N4	Louisbourg	G10	Presqu'ile	D9	Vaughan	K6
		East River	K6	Louisdale	H9	Preston	K7	Victoria Beach	K4
		East River St. Mary's	I8	Low Landing	L5	Prospect	L6	Walden	K6
		Eastern Passage	K7	Lower Argyle	N4	Pubnico	N4	Wallace	H7
		Eastville	I7	Lower Barney's River	H8	Pubnico Beach	O4	Wallace Bay	G7
		Economy	I6	Lower Economy	I6	Pugwash	G6	Wallace Ridge	H7
		Ecum Secum	J8	Lower Ship Harbour	K7	Pugwash Junction	H6	Wallace Station	H7
		Eden Lake	I8	Lower West Pubnico	O4	Queensport	I9	Walton	I6
		Elderbank	K7	Lower Wood Harbour	O4	Rawdon	J6	Wards Brook	I6
		Ellershouse	J6	Lunenburg	L6	Rawdon Gold Mines	J6	Waterford	L4
		Elmsdale	J7	Lynn	I6	Reserve Mines	F10	Waterloo	L6
		Enfield	J7	Lyons Brook	H7	River Bourgeois	N9	Waternish	I8
		Englishtown	F9	Mabou	F8	River Hebert	H6	Waterville	K7
		Eskasoni	G9	Maccan	H6	River John	H7	Waverley	K7
		Eureka	H7	Mahone Bay	L6	River Philip	H6	Weaver Settlement	L4
		Falmouth	J6	Main-à-Dieu	F10	Riverport	L6	Wedgeport	N4
		Finlayson	F9	Maitland	I7	Ross Ferry	F9	Wentworth	H7
		Five Islands	I6	Maitland Bridge	L5	Rossway	L4	Wentworth Centre	H7
		Florence	F9	Malagash	H7	Round Hill	K5	West Arichat	H9
		Folly Lake	H7	Malagash Station	H7	Sable River	N5	West Bay Road	G9
		Forties Settlement	K6	Malignant Cove	G8	Sackville	K7	West Berlin	M6
		Fourchu	G10	Mapleton	H6	Salmon River	M4	W. Branch R. John	H7
		Fox Harbour	G7	Marble Mountain	G9	Salmon River	I7	West Brook	I6
		Framboise	G9	Margaree Forks	F9	Salmon River Road	G9	West Jeddore	K7
		Freeport	L4	Margaree Harbour	E9	Salt Springs	H7	West Pubnico	N4
		Gabarus	G10	Margaree Valley	E9	Sambro	L7	West River	H7
		Gabarus Lake	G10	Margaretsville	J5	Sand Point	H9	West River Station	H6
		Gays River	J7	Marion Bridge	G10	Sand River	I5	Westchester Station	H6
		Georgeville	G8	Marshy Hope	H8	Sandford	N4	Western Shore	L6
		Giant Lake	I8	Martins River	L6	Sandy Cove	L4	Westport	M4
		Gibraltar	J7					Westville	H7

Place	Grid
Weymouth	L4
Weymouth Falls	L4
White Point	M5
Whitehead	I9
Whites Lake	L6
Whycocomagh	G9
Wilmot	J5
Windsor	J6
Windsor Forks	J6
Windsor Junction	K7
Wolfville	J6
Woodvale	M4
Wreck Cove	E9
Yarmouth	N4

PRINCE EDWARD ISLAND

Place	Grid
Abram-Village	F6
Alberton	D6
Baltic	E8
Bear River	F8
Belle River	G7
Bonshaw	F7
Borden	F6
Brackley Beach	F7
Breadalbane	F7
Bunbury	F7
Campbellton	E6
Cardigan	F7
Cavendish	E7
Central Bedeque	F6
Charlottetown	F7
Cornwall	F7
Crapaud	F7
De Sable	F7
East Point	E8
Egmont Bay	F6
Eldon	G7
Ellerslie	E6
Elmira	E8
Elmsdale	D6
Fortune Bridge	F8
Freetown	F6
Georgetown	F7
Hunter River	F7
Kensington	F6
Keppoch	F7
Kinkora	F6
Knutsford	E6
Little Pond	F8
Malpeque	E6
Miminegash	D6
Miscouche	F6
Mont-Carmel	F6
Montague	F7
Morell	F7
Mount Stewart	F7
Murray Harbour	G7
Murray River	G7
Naufrage	E8
New Glasgow	F7
New London	F7
North Lake	E8
North Rustico	F7
O'Leary	E6
Parkdale	F7
Pinette	G7
Pooles Corner	F7
Portage	E6
Rocky Point	F7
Rollo Bay	F8
Sherwood	F7
Souris	F8
Southport	F7
St-Chrysostome	E6
St. Eleanors	F6
St. Louis	D6
St. Peters	F7
St. Teresa	F7
Stanhope	F7
Stanley Bridge	F7
Sturgeon	G7
Summerside	F6
Tignish	D6
Tyne Valley	E6
Vernon Bridge	F7
Vernon River	F7
Victoria	F7
Wellington	F6
West Devon	E6
Wilmot	F6
Winslow	F7
Wood Islands	G7

A distance matrix is found on Gazetteer-4.

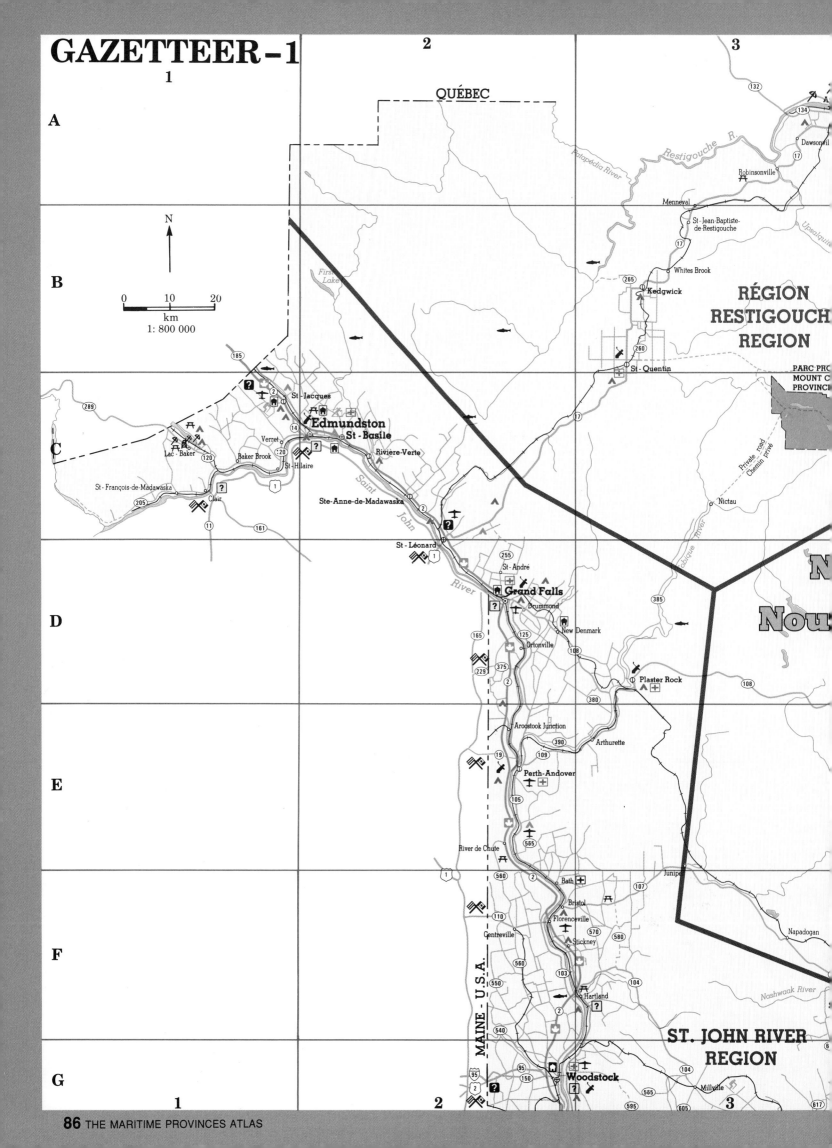

GAZETTEER-1

1   **2**   **3**

QUÉBEC

N

0   10   20
km
1 : 800 000

A

B

Patapédia River   Restigouche R.   A
132
134
Dawsonvil
Robinsonville   17
Menneval
St-Jean-Baptiste-
de-Restigouche
Whites Brook   17
265   Kedgwick   Upsalquite

**RÉGION
RESTIGOUCH
REGION**

185
St-Quentin   260
PARC PRO
MOUNT C
PROVINCE

C

289
St-Jacques   2
14   **Edmundston**
St-Basile
Lac-Baker   120   Verret   20   Rivière-Verte   17
Baker Brook   St-Hilaire   Nictau
St-François-de-Madawaska   205   Clair   1
11   161   Ste-Anne-de-Madawaska   2

Saint   John   River   Private road
Chemin privé

D

St-Léonard   1
255   St-André
Grand Falls
Drummond
New Denmark
165   125   Ortonville   108
229   375   2   380   Plaster Rock   108
385

**N
Nou**

E

Aroostook Junction
390   Arthurette
19   109
Perth-Andover
105

F

565
River de Chute   1
560   2   Bath   Juniper
107
Bristol
110   Florenceville   Napadogan
Centreville   570   580
Stickney   103   104
560
MAINE - U.S.A.   540   Hartland   Nashwaak River

**ST. JOHN RIVER
REGION**

G

95   95   150
2   **Woodstock**   104   Millville   605   617
595

1   **2**   **3**

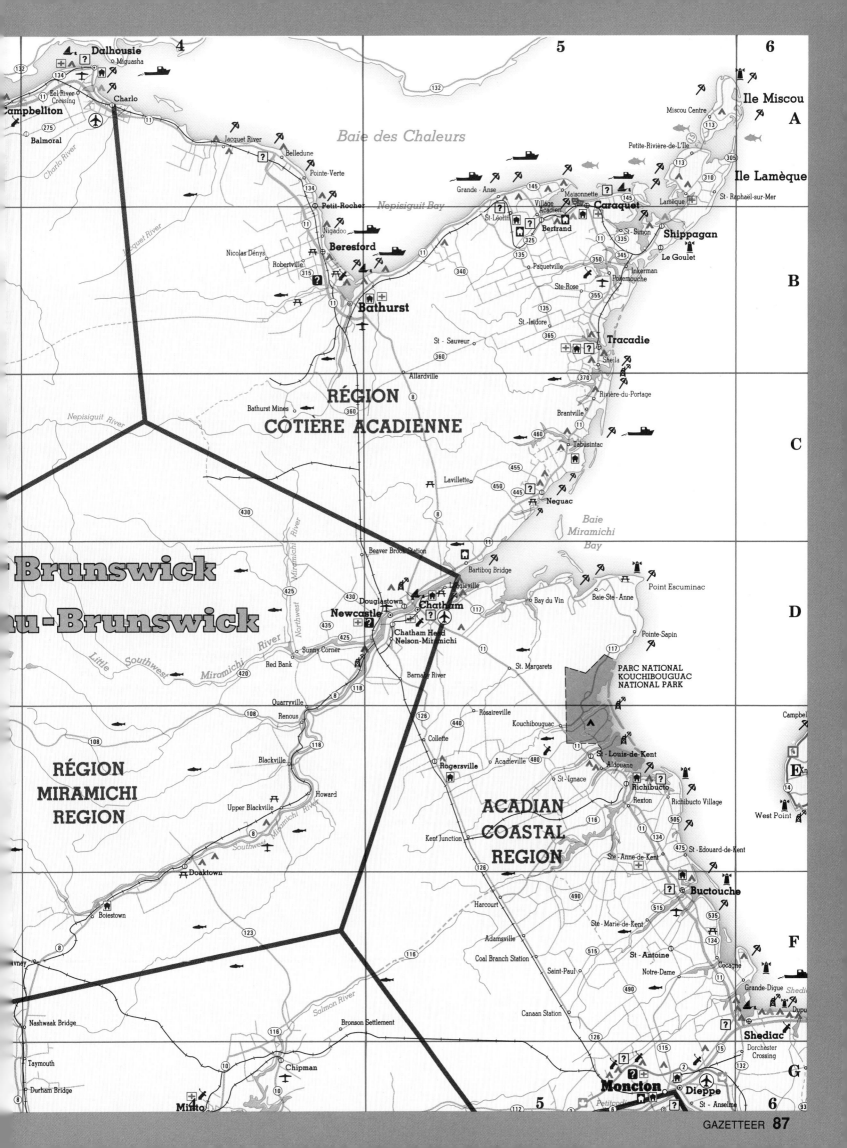

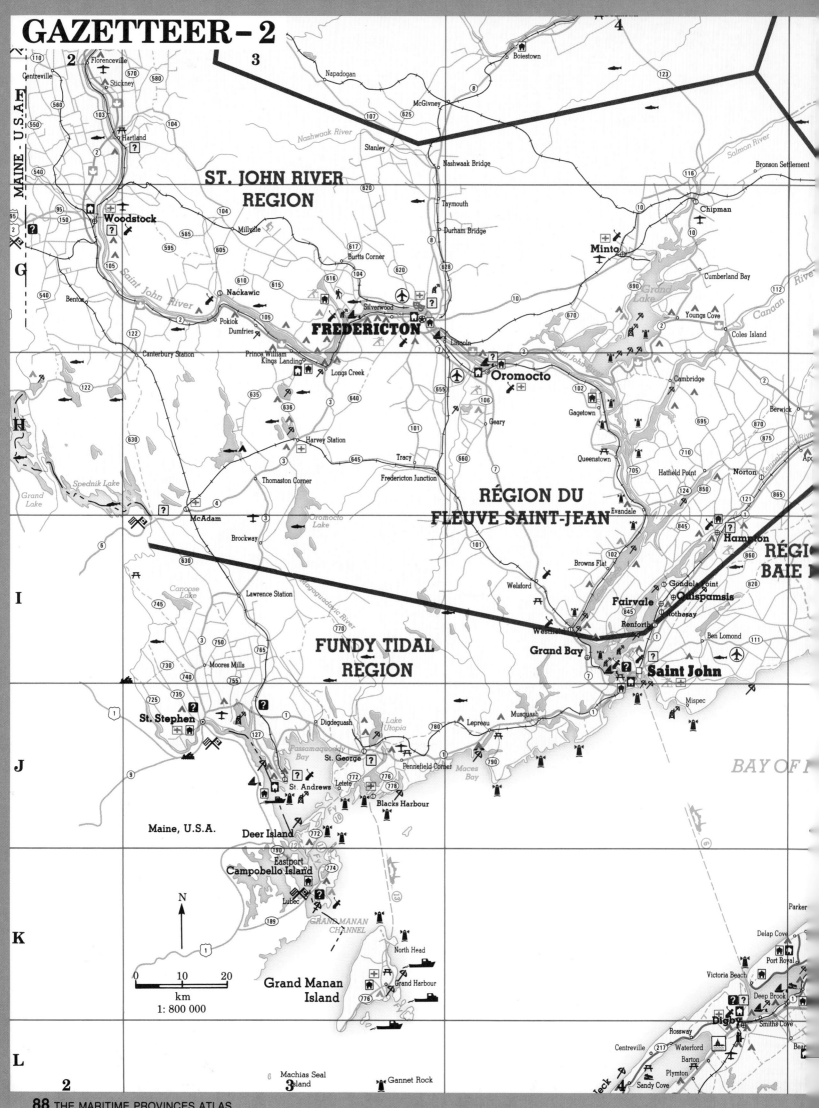

GAZETTEER - 2

ST. JOHN RIVER REGION

RÉGION DU FLEUVE SAINT-JEAN

FUNDY TIDAL REGION

Maine, U.S.A.

N

0   10   20
km
1: 800 000

Florenceville
Centreville
Stickney
Hartland
Woodstock
Benton
Nackawic
Pokiok
Dumfries
Canterbury Station
Prince William
Kings Landing
Longs Creek
Millville
Burtts Corner
FREDERICTON
Silverwood
Nashwaak Bridge
Stanley
Nashwaak River
Napadogan
McGivney
Boiestown
Taymouth
Durham Bridge
Lincoln
Oromocto
Geary
Harvey Station
Tracy
Fredericton Junction
Thomaston Corner
McAdam
Brockway
Oromocto Lake
Lawrence Station
Canoose Lake
Moores Mills
St. Stephen
St. Andrews
Deer Island
Eastport
Campobello Island
Lubec
Grand Manan Island
North Head
Grand Harbour
Machias Seal Island
Gannet Rock
Digdeguash
Lake Utopia
St. George
Letete
Pennfield Corner
Maces Bay
Blacks Harbour
Lepreau
Musquash
Grand Bay
Saint John
Mispec
Ben Lomond
Westfield
Renforth
Fairvale
Quispamsis
Rothesay
Gondola Point
Hampton
Welsford
Browns Flat
Evandale
Hatfield Point
Norton
Queenstown
Gagetown
Cambridge
Berwick
Youngs Cove
Coles Island
Cumberland Bay
Minto
Chipman
Grand Lake
Bronson Settlement
Salmon River
Spednik Lake
Grand Lake
Passamaquoddy Bay
GRAND MANAN CHANNEL
BAY OF FUNDY
Delap Cove
Port Royal
Victoria Beach
Deep Brook
Digby
Smiths Cove
Rossway
Centreville
Waterford
Barton
Plymton
Sandy Cove
Parker

MAINE - U.S.A.

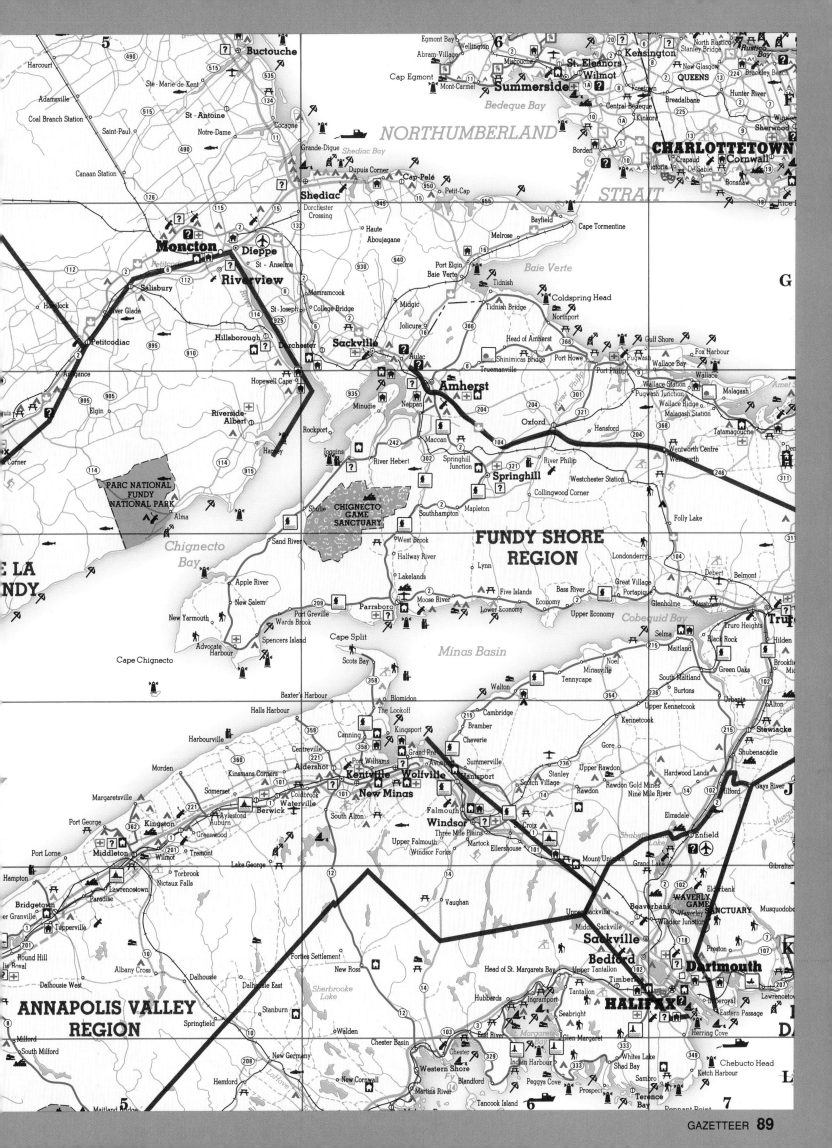

C

D

North Cape

Tignish

14

12

Miminegash

St. Louis

Cape Kildare

Elmsdale

Alberton

Campbellton

Knutsford

O'Leary

Cascumpec Bay

E

West Devon

Portage

12

Ellerslie

2

123

PRINCE

Tyne Valley

GULF OF ST. LAWRENCE

Prince Edward Island
Ile-du-Prince-Edouard

Egmont Bay

St. Chrysostome

11

Egmont Bay C.

Wellington

12

Malpeque

20

Malpeque Bay

New London

Cavendish

Stanley Bridge

North Rustico

PRINCE EDWARD ISLAND NATIONAL PARK

Rustico Bay

Shipwreck Pt.

Naufrage

Long Pt.

16

16

St. Peters

Bear River

218

Morell

312

Rollo Bay

Souris

Abram-Village

Miscouche

Kensington

Cap Egmont

Mont-Carmel

St. Eleanors

Wilmot

Summerside

Bedeque Bay

New Glasgow

QUEENS

Freetown

224

Breadalbane

Brackley Beach

Hunter River

2

7

Stanhope

Tracadie Bay

6

Mount Stewart

25

KINGS

St. Teresa

313

Fortune Bridge

310

Little Pond

Spry Pt.

F

NORTHUMBERLAND

Shediac Bay

Dupuis Corner

Cap-Pelé

950

Petit-Cap

945

955

15

Central Bedeque

1A

Kinkora

225

10

Borden

Winsloe

Sherwood

9

CHARLOTTETOWN

Victoria

Crapaud

De Sable

Cornwall

Bonshaw

19

Parkdale

Bunbury

Southport

Keppoch

Rocky Point

Vernon River

Vernon Bridge

3

22

Pooles Corner

Cardigan

311

Boughton Is.

Cardigan Bay

Georgetown

Panmure Island

Montague

24

315

17A

Sturgeon

17

Rice Pt.

19

Hillsborough Bay

Pt. Prim

209

Pinette

Eldon

23

315

Murray River

17

18

Cape Bear

Murray Harbour

G

Baie Verte

Shediac Bay

930

940

Bayfield

Melrose

Cape Tormentine

Port Elgin

Baie Verte

Tidnish

Midgic

Jolicure

16

366

Tidnish Bridge

Coldspring Head

Northport

Belle River

Wood Islands

Pictou Island

H

ackville

Aulac

2

935

Minudie

Nappan

Amherst

242

302

Maccan

2

204

Oxford

321

Hansford

204

368

Springhill Junction

321

River Philip

Springhill

Westchester Station

Collingwood Corner

Mapleton

Southhampton

CHIGNECTO GAME SANCTUARY

West Brook

Halfway River

Lynn

Lakelands

Parrsboro

358

Moose River

Five Islands

Bass River

Economy

Lower Economy

Upper Economy

Cobequid Bay

Head of Amherst

366

Shinimicas Bridge

Port Howe

Truemanville

301

Pugwash Junction

Gulf Shore

Pugwash

Wallace Bay

Fox Harbour

Port Philip

6

Wallace Station

Wallace

Cape John

Seafoam

Caribou Island

Amet Sound

Malagash

Wallace Ridge

Malagash Station

Toney River

River John

Caribou River

1

Caribou

246

Tatamagouche

Wentworth Centre

Wentworth

Denmark

West Branch River John

256

Lyons Brook

Pictou

106

Trenton

Merigomish

Lower Barney

Avonc

Lismore

245

Earltown

West River

Scotsburn

Salt Springs

Greenhill

West River Station

FUNDY SHORE REGION

Great Village

Portapique

Glenholme

Masstown

Debert

Belmont

Folly Lake

311

Kemptown

West River Station

104

New Glasgow

Sutherland River

Thorburn

NORTH

Westville

Stellarton

Eureka

Hopewell

Bridgeville

Blue Mountain

247

Ed

Nova Scotia
Nouvelle-Ecoss

I

Cape Split

Scots Bay

358

Blomidon

The Lookoff

Minas Basin

Walton

Noel

Minasville

Tennycape

354

Maitland

Selma

215

Black Rock

South Maitland

Burtons

236

Urbania

Green Oaks

Brookfield

Middle Stewiacke

102

Upper Stewiacke

Truro

Truro Heights

Hilden

Eastville

LISCOMB

GAME

SANCTUARY

J

ip

Kingsport

Cambridge

215

Bramber

6

Kennetcook

Upper Kennetcook

215

Stewiacke

Alton

Upper Musquodoboit

7

324